VENICE
THE ART OF LIVING

Texts
TOTO BERGAMO ROSSI
LYDIA FASOLI

Photographs
MARIE PIERRE MOREL

Foreword by
JUDE LAW

RIZZOLI
NEW YORK

New York · Paris · London · Milan

PREVIOUS SPREAD: A view of the Giudecca: at the center the Church of
Santa Maria della Visitazione, also known as Chiesa delle Zitelle;
Hotel Bauer Palladio; and on the right Casa dei Tre Oci and Villa F,
previously Casa Frollo.
LEFT TO RIGHT, TOP TO BOTTOM: *Salatini* and *tarallucci*; the Dogana da
Mar; the recipe book of the Soccol family; the garden of Villa F;
the dining room on the ground floor of Villa Foscari; a terrace at
Gradenigo Ancilotto; polenta and *schie*; the pier of the Piazzetta;
zucchini blossom flowers.

TABLE OF CONTENTS

FOREWORD

Like many English travelers on the Grand Tour in the eighteenth century, I too was struck by the beauty of Italy, enjoying the sun that shows up so rarely in Northern Europe, that gentle Mediterranean climate that certainly must have influenced the character of the various people who have populated the Italian peninsula in the last two thousand years. It was a few years ago, when I was working on the set of *The Talented Mr. Ripley*, that I began enjoying Italian *art de vivre*. Like Sir William Hamilton—the British ambassador to the Neapolitan court of the Bourbons—I too have gotten lost in the streets of Naples, among the ruins of Herculaneum and Pompeii and in the labyrinth of alleys of Procida and Ischia, and have tasted a *mozzarella di bufala* from the valley of Paestum, garnished with that basil that smells so intensely only in southern Italy. More recently, while shooting some scenes for *The Young Pope* in Venice, I had a chance to discover another side of this city, a more intimate, private, and authentic side, outside of the usual tourist experience. Like Lord Byron, I was unable to resist the charm of the Serenissima and have visited museums, churches, and palaces that are off the normal tourist routes. Among these, thanks to the authors of this book, I also saw some of the secret residences that are revealed here. Residences that may seem uninhabited from the outside, but inside are lavishly furnished and decorated with marvelous frescoes and stuccoes. I was speechless when I watched the Historical Regatta from Casa Chiari Gaggia's terrace that overlooks the Grand Canal, opposite the iconic Basilica della Salute, sipping a home-made Bellini; or when I discovered that Gabriele D'Annunzio had set some of the pages of his famous novel *The Flame* in the garden of my friend Toto Bergamo Rossi, even while Henry James was writing *The Aspern Papers* in the neighboring garden and palazzo.

As an honorary member of the Venetian Heritage Foundation I am happy to promote not only the protection of the immense heritage of Venetian art, but also the Venetian lifestyle which, notwithstanding the centuries gone by, continues to captivate visitors with its hospitality, elegance, and culinary tradition.

Jude Law

INTRODUCTION

"So much has already been said and printed about Venice, that I shall not be circumstantial in my description, but shall only say how it struck me [...]. It was for no idle fancy that this race fled to these islands; it was no mere whim which impelled those who followed to combine with them; necessity taught them to look for security in a highly disadvantageous situation that afterward became most advantageous, enduing them with talent when the whole northern world was immersed in gloom. Their increase and their wealth were a necessary consequence." This is how, in 1786, Goethe opens his description of his stay in Venice in *Letters From Italy*, where he spent time visiting the buildings designed by Palladio and going to the crowded city theaters at night, where the comedies of Gozzi and Goldoni were being represented. Almost in the same years, the exiled Giacomo Casanova wrote nostalgically about his hometown. Among the many things, Casanova spoke of the spaghetti with clams and the Venetian polenta, dishes impossible to find in the castle of Dux in Bohemia, where he spent the last few years of his life, far away from his beloved Venetian lagoon.

The present volume describes twelve Venetian residences, some of them visited by Goethe and Casanova. There are luxurious patrician palaces, lived in by friends who still host with elegance and style, and have offered to share their recipes with our readers; other houses are in the lagoon, where the landscape and the old hunting and fishing traditions have remained the same over the centuries and one can still see the scenes captured in the paintings of Carpaccio and Longhi. In these natural enclaves, one can also enjoy the typical dishes of these timeless localities. The last residences in the book are the country villas, beautiful mansions built by aristocratic Venetian families in the country to serve both as holiday resorts and as the center of their farming activities. In the villas, the owners have shown us around and opened for us the gates of their magnificent gardens. They have also shared with us their old family recipes, moved by our same desire to promote and preserve Venetian art and culture, even while dining.

Toto Bergamo Rossi and Lydia Fasoli

An elegant house on the Grand Canal

PALAZZETTO ALVISI GAGGIA

T he oldest section of the three buildings that presently comprise the Gaggia home dates to the first half of the seventeenth century and was built by the patrician Giustinian family on property previously owned by the Michiel family. In 1876, the palazzetto was chosen as their Italian residence by Arthur and Katherine Bronson, two wealthy Americans with an interest in the arts. Mrs. Bronson regularly hosted guests and international travelers in her salon, among which were Henry James and Mrs. Bronson's close friend the poet Robert Browning, who lived in Ca' Rezzonico, the palace owned by his son, Pen.

In the 1920s, senator of the Italian kingdom Achille Gaggia (along with Vittorio Cini and Giuseppe Volpi, one of the moguls of Italian economy and industry in the early twentieth century) purchased Palazzetto Alvisi and commissioned the redecoration and expansion of the building to Count Mantegazza, a famous architect.

A number of minor buildings were first purchased and then demolished, making it possible to build the splendid terrace on the second floor and the side wing, currently occupied by the salon-library.

Other important work was carried out: the grand stairway, the stucco decorations on the second floor, the beautiful floors, and the furniture and objects, still present today, all which impart an aura of great elegance to the residence.

The present owners, the grandchildren of senator Gaggia, still give splendid receptions. In the magnificent dining room, a fabulous set of plates by the Venetian manufactory Cozzi dating to 1760 is exhibited.

Everything is perfect in the Chiari Gaggia residence, from the soft lighting to the excellent meals, served on splendid eighteenth-century porcelain tableware.

Finally there is the terrace, offering a breathtaking view of the Basilica della Salute directly opposite, while on the left visitors can admire the facade of the church of San Giorgio Maggiore by Andrea Palladio.

ABOVE: The cupola of the Basilica della Salute reflected on the waters of the Grand Canal, in front of the palace.
OPPOSITE: The Basilica della Salute as seen from the *sala della loggia*. On the sides, two lacquered Venetian wood sculptures from the eighteenth century.
FOLLOWING SPREAD: In the center of the *sala della loggia* is a precious hexagonal neoclassical table, probably Russian, on which a collection of engraved Murano glass is exhibited. The chandelier, also from Murano, dates to the eighteenth century.

OPPOSITE: The antechamber of the second floor is decorated in eighteenth-century-style stuccoes. On the wall, a view of Bacino di San Marco and to the side, a *gueridon*, of carved and gilded wood, supports an eighteenth-century Chinese vase.

LEFT (BOTTOM) AND ABOVE: The *sala cinese* or Chinese room, so called because of the stucco *chinoiserie* decorating the ceiling. Almost all the furniture, like the *magot* in lacquered wood, dates to the eighteenth century.

OPPOSITE AND BELOW: The walls and the curtains of the *sala cinese* are made of pale pink tapestries in the eighteenth-century style. Snacks are always served on eighteenth-century silver dishes. The glasses are made of blown Murano glass.

SALATINI BIANCHI E ROSSI

Red and White Savory Tartlets

MAKES ABOUT ONE DOZEN TARTLETS

Pastry base:
· 2 cups (9 oz. / 250 g) all-purpose flour
· 1 stick (4 ½ oz. / 125 g) butter, at a warm room temperature, diced

Toppings:
· 1 onion
· 1 tablespoon olive oil
· 1 piece Fontina cheese or 1 ball fresh mozzarella
· 1 anchovy fillet, packed in oil
· Tomato passata or crushed tomatoes, blended
· 1 sprig thyme
· Salt

Make the pastry base: combine the flour and butter to make a smooth dough. If necessary, add a little water so that it comes together. Shape into a disk and store in the refrigerator, covered in plastic wrap, for 30 minutes.

Preheat the oven to 350°F (180°C). Line a baking sheet with parchment paper.

Make the tartlets: Roll the dough out thinly, and, using a cookie cutter, cut out small rounds. Chop the onion and sauté it in the olive oil. Cut the cheese into cubes and the anchovy fillet into very small pieces.

Top the pastry rounds with a little of the tomato passata, a cube of cheese, and a piece of anchovy fillet; a little sautéed onion seasoned with salt; or two cubes of cheese seasoned with some thyme leaves.

Bake for 15 minutes and serve warm.

BELOW, RIGHT, AND OPPOSITE: The kitchen was restored by Andrea Chiari Gaggia. The furniture is the work of the traditional Capovilla manufactory in Venice. The cook Elena, and her husband Pietro, the butler, take superb care of this historical residence.

MAFALDE ALLE CANOCE

Mafalde Pasta with Mantis Shrimp

SERVES 4
· 3 lb. (1½ kg) mantis shrimp
· 1 lb. (500 g) mafalde, mafaldine, or fettucine pasta
· ¼ cup (60 ml) olive oil, divided
· 1 bunch flat-leaf parsley, finely chopped
· Salt and freshly ground pepper

Wash the mantis shrimp well. Using a pair of scissors, carefully cut the shells and extract the flesh, taking care not to damage it. Cut it into pieces. Bring a large pot of salted water to a boil. Add the pasta and cook according to the instructions.

In a large skillet, heat one tablespoon of the olive oil and rapidly sauté the pieces of shrimp. Stir in the chopped parsley.

Drain the pasta, reserving a ladleful of the cooking liquid. Add the sautéed shrimp pieces to the pasta with the remaining olive oil, and incorporate the cooking liquid for added flavor.

Mantis shrimp, canoce, are small crustaceans that are caught at night. Their taste is somewhat reminiscent of lobsters.

LEFT (TOP) AND OPPOSITE: In the dining room, white-lacquered consoles with gilded reliefs in Louis XVI style adorn the walls on the sides of the doors. The carafes and the goblets in blown Murano glass are by Venini.
LEFT (BOTTOM): The Basilica della Salute, seen from the windows of Senator Gaggia's study.

SFORMATO DI RISO AL TORREGGIANO

Rice Timbale with Squab

SERVES 4

· 1 onion
· 3 tablespoons olive oil, divided
· 1 or 2 prepared squab, with the giblets
· ¾ cup (200 ml) red wine
· 4 cups (1 liter) chicken broth, or enough
  to cook the rice
· 2 lb. (1 kg) round-grained rice
· ¼ cup (2 oz. / 50 g) Parmigiano Reggiano, grated
· 1 egg, lightly beaten
· 3⅓ cups (7 oz. / 200 g) fresh breadcrumbs,
  or 1½ cups (7 oz. / 200 g) packaged breadcrumbs
· Butter for the mold
· Salt and freshly ground pepper

Prepare the squab meat: Chop the onion. In a large pot, sauté the onion with 2 tablespoons of the olive oil. Color the squab on all sides. Pour in the wine and allow it to evaporate, then season with salt and pepper. Cover with the lid, and reduce the heat to low. Continue to cook the meat, pouring the juices over regularly, for about 20 minutes. In a skillet, heat the remaining olive oil and sauté the giblets for 10 minutes. When the meat is cool enough to handle, tear it off in small pieces.

Prepare the rice timbale: Bring the chicken broth to a boil and cook the rice at a full rolling boil in it for 16 minutes. Drain, allow to cool to warm, and stir in the egg and grated cheese.

Preheat the oven to 450°F (230°C).

Butter a mold 7½ inches (19 cm) in diameter and 4½ inches (11 cm) deep. Line the mold with the breadcrumbs. Cover the base and sides with a ¾ inch (2 cm) layer of rice. Cover with squab meat. Create a small hole in the middle of the meat and insert the giblets. Cover with the remaining rice. Bake for 35 minutes.

Turn the timbale onto a platter and serve hot.

PREVIOUS SPREAD: The art of entertaining at the Gaggia home has been handed down through four generations. The hand-embroidered nineteenth-century tablecloth is from Burano. The porcelain from the Maissen manufactory and the silver English chandeliers are both from the eighteenth century.
OPPOSITE AND BELOW: The *timballo* is served on an antique silver serving dish and the San Marco cutlery set has the typical three-pointed forks. The carafes are by Venini and date to the 1940s.

ZABAIONE

Zabaglione

SERVES 4
· 3 egg yolks
· ½ cup (3½ oz. / 100 g) sugar
· 1¼ cups (300 ml) Moscato wine or other Muscato-based dessert wine

Whisk the egg yolks with the sugar. Gradually drizzle in the Moscato, whisking continuously, until the mixture is frothy.

Pour into a heatproof bowl, and place over a hot water bath set over low heat. Continue to whisk the mixture until it increases in volume.

Allow to cool to lukewarm and pour into bowls. Serve with *baicoli*, traditional Venetian cookies.

GELATO E PASSATO DI KAKI

Vanilla Ice Cream with Persimmon Coulis

SERVES 6
· 4 egg yolks
· Scant ½ cup (3 oz. / 80 g) sugar
· 1 cup (250 ml) milk
· ⅔ cup (150 ml) whipping cream
· Seeds of 1 vanilla bean
· 4 ripe persimmons

Make the ice cream: Briskly whisk the egg yolks with the sugar until frothy. Whisk in the milk, cream, and vanilla seeds. Pour the mixture into the bowl of an ice cream maker, and make ice cream according to instructions. Place the churned mixture in the freezer for about 30 minutes.

Make the persimmon coulis: Scoop all of the flesh out of the persimmons and blend until smooth.

Serve the ice cream with the coulis.

LEFT: The dining room by candlelight with a precious antique Burano tablecloth.
OPPOSITE: The silver pineapple is a pepper grinder by Missiaglia, while the ice cream bowl and the San Marco dinner set are both from the 1950s.

RICE

Rice is a major element of Venetian cuisine. It was introduced into Italy in the fifteenth century, and the sediments of the estuary and humid environment make it an ideal place to cultivate the grains. Superfine carnaroli rice is one of the varieties best suited for preparing risotto. Today in Venice, the Bastienello family, who produce La Fagiano rice, grows a particularly fine-quality carnaroli, even calling on specialists from Vietnam for help in the harvest. The rice is entirely hand-picked and sold in specialty grocery stores in the city. Every single home cook has his or her own way of preparing risotto. The secret lies in selecting a single main ingredient to highlight, so that the flavors of the rice can shine through. November 21 is the feast of the Madonna della Salute, and it is customary to prepare a risotto dish *en cavroman*, with a pesto of Middle Eastern spices accompanied by *castradina*, or mutton that has been cooked three times. It is eaten at home, on boats, and is served as street food on this saint's day.

An aristocratic palace

PALAZZO GRADENIGO IN RIO MARIN

Ancilotto Gradenigo Wing

The origin of this palace dates to the middle of the sixteenth century. In the second half of the seventeenth century, the Gradenigos, one of the most ancient and renowned families in Venetian nobility, decided to double the size of the building and entrusted the work to Baldassare Longhena, the well-known architect who designed the Basilica della Salute. After Longhena's death, the project was carried out by his student Domenico Margutti.

The palace was famous for its collections of paintings, its rich library, and above all, for its gardens, which up to 1922 were the largest in the city. During the Carnival of 1768, bull hunts were organized, and later, memorable feasts in honor of Eugene de Bauharnais.

At the end of the nineteenth century, Gabriele D'Annunzio set part of his famous and scandalous novel *Il fuoco* (The Flame) among the shrubs of the Gradenigo gardens. Around the same time, Henry James set his short story *The Aspern Papers* in the adjacent gardens.

In the gardens, there was also a riding ground and a stable, which in 1750 numbered no less than thirty horses and a few carriages.

The wing on the second floor overlooking the garden is presently inhabited by the Ancilotto Gradenigo family.

All sections of the wing are decorated with stuccoes and frescoes, and the rooms contain many important historical documents and memorabilia associated with this ancient ducal family.

In the room called *sala degli stucchi*, there is a gallery of portraits of important members of the family set among rocaille decorations, among which is the portrait of Pietro Gradenigo, the doge famous for having passed the law known as the Serrata del Maggior Consiglio in 1297.

The red hall (or fireplace hall) is enriched by a great oval canvas painted by Giacomo Guarana, located in the center of the ceiling and surrounded by stucco.

A small boudoir, adorned with elegant stuccoes, connects the halls to the bedrooms. Here one can still breathe the magical atmosphere of the elegant soirees of eighteenth-century Venice.

PREVIOUS SPREAD: The *sala dei dogi* (room of the doges) is decorated with polychrome stuccoes dating to the mid-eighteenth century, framing portraits on canvas of various doges belonging to the Gradenigo family, as well as other important members of the family. The room is set up as a game room and furnished with Venetian furniture in Louis XV style.
BELOW: Detail of the portrait of Doge Pietro Gradenigo, attributed to Giacomo Guarana.
OPPOSITE: The ceiling of the boudoir of Palazzo Gradenigo, used as a small living room, decorated with sophisticated stuccoes from the late seventeenth century, while the walls and wood floors are the result of the elegant redecoration of this wing of the palace that took place in the latter half of the nineteenth century.

PORRI AGLI SCAMPI

Leeks with Scampi

SERVES 4
· 3 leeks
· 1 tablespoon (20 g) butter
· 6 scampi (Norway lobster)
· Salt and freshly ground pepper
· A little freshly ground nutmeg

Wash the leeks and slice them finely. Sauté them in the butter for at least 10 minutes, or until softened, occassionally stirring them. In the meantime, shell the scampi and cut into thin slices.

When the leeks are done, stir in the sliced scampi. Season with salt and pepper. Stir in a small pinch of freshly ground nutmeg. Serve warm.

SCAMPI IN AGRODOLCE

Sweet and Sour Scampi

SERVES 4
· 1 lb. (500 g) scampi (Norway lobster)
· ¾ cup (200 ml) white wine vinegar
· 1½ sweet onions, sliced into rounds
· 2 bay leaves
· ¼ cup (60 ml) extra virgin olive oil
· 1 teaspoon sugar
· Salt and freshly ground pepper

Bring 2 cups (500 ml) of water to a boil.

Shell the prawns and throw them into the water. Allow to simmer gently for 5 minutes, then drain.

Pour the vinegar into a mixing bowl and add the onions, bay leaves, olive oil, and sugar. Immerse the scampi in the mixture to cool them. Season with salt and pepper. Allow to marinate for 12 hours in the refrigerator.

FOLLOWING PAGES: The 1950s kitchen, which has remained practically the same, is where traditional Venetian dishes are prepared. The daughters of Countess Ancilotto Gradenigo take religious care of the old notebook containing the family recipes.

Shrimp with White Polenta

SERVES 4
- ½ lb (8 oz.) shrimp
- Juice of ½ lemon
- 1⅔ cups (400 ml) milk
- 1¾ cups (4 oz. / 400 g) fine white cornmeal
- 1 bunch flat-leaf parsley, chopped
- A drizzle of extra virgin olive oil
- Salt and freshly ground pepper

Place the shrimp in a pot of boiling water and cook for 2 minutes. Drain well and drizzle them with the lemon juice.

In a large pot, bring 4 cups (1 liter) of water to a boil with the milk. Pour in the cornmeal and reduce the heat to low. Stirring constantly, cook for at least 30 minutes. The polenta should not become too thick, but remain slightly fluid.

Spread the polenta in a serving dish and arrange the shrimp over it. Sprinkle with the chopped parsley, and drizzle with olive oil. Season with salt and pepper and serve.

LEFT (TOP): Detail of the walnut door of the *sala rossa*, with glass handle. (BOTTOM): Oval portraits of distinguished members of the Gradenigo family adorn the walls of the *sala dei dogi*.
OPPOSITE: Polenta and *schie*, a classical autumnal Venetian dish, presented on a ceramic Bassano dish shaped like a cabbage leaf. The *schie* are fished only in autumn. The white polenta is less known than the yellow variety and is mostly used in Venetian cuisine.

OPPOSITE: Figs gathered in the garden are displayed on a dish of Faenza majolica of the 1920s, accompanied by a sweet white wine.

LEFT: The kitchen furniture is hand painted and lined with an artisanal paper from Florence. The cupboard contains a collection of tin and copper cake molds. On the lower shelf, a porcelain tea set by Ginori from the 1920s.

ABOVE: A harmonious combination of cream and blue colors imparts an old-fashioned atmosphere to the kitchen. On the table, a silver tray by Missiaglia and a tin carafe.

PAN DI SPAGNA AL MELONE

Layered Sponge Cake with Pastry Cream and Melon

SERVES 4

Pastry Cream:
· 4 egg yolks
· Scant ⅓ cup (2 oz. / 60 g) sugar
· ½ cup (2 oz. / 60 g) all-purpose flour
· ½ cup (2 oz. / 50 g) almond flour
· 2 cups (500 ml) milk
· Seeds of 1 vanilla bean

Make the pastry cream: Using an electric beater or a whisk, whip the egg yolks with the sugar until the mixture is pale and thick. Whisk in the

flour and almond flour, and drizzle in a little milk, whisking until the mixture is more fluid.

In a saucepan over medium heat, heat the remaining milk. Stir in the vanilla seeds. When the milk is warm, stir in the egg yolk mixture. Continue stirring until the mixture thickens. Remove from the heat, let cool, then press plastic wrap directly on to the surface. Refrigerate until needed.

Genoese Sponge Cake:
· 1 cup plus 2 tablespoons (5 oz. / 150 g) all-purpose flour
· 1¼ teaspoons (5 g) baking powder
· 5 eggs
· ¾ cup (5 oz. / 150 g) sugar
· 1 cantaloupe melon

Icing:
· 1 cup (5¼ oz. / 150 g) confectioners' sugar
· 4 tablespoons hot water

Preheat the oven to 285°F (140°C). Butter a 10 x 14-inch (25 x 35 cm) cake pan.

Combine the flour with the baking powder. Separate the eggs. Using a stand mixer or an electric beater, whisk the egg whites until they hold soft peaks. Add the sugar and whisk further. Reduce the speed and whisk in all of the egg yolks at once, and then the flour with the baking powder until just combined.

Pour the batter into the prepared cake pan, smooth the surface, and bake for 20 minutes, or until a cake tester comes out clean. Allow to cool to lukewarm in the pan, then turn onto a rack. When the cake has cooled, use a long, serrated knife to cut it into three sections horizontally.

To assemble the cake: Finely slice the melon. Spread a layer of pastry cream over the first layer of Genoese sponge cake and arrange half of the melon slices over it. Carefully place the second layer of sponge cake over that, and repeat to cover with pastry cream and melon slices. Place the last layer of sponge on top.

Make the icing and decorate: Whisk the icing sugar with the water until smooth and spread over the cake. Refrigerate for 12 hours.

A historical palace and a secret garden

PALAZZO GRADENIGO IN RIO MARIN

Bergamo Rossi Wing

One arrives at Palazzo Gradenigo from the bank of the same name, going through a neoclassical arch surmounted by a coat of arms with triumphant sculpted soldiers. Like the other wing of the palace, this wing is also decorated with stuccoes and frescoes from different periods.

The walls of the entrance represent a virtuoso performance of the art of stucco in 1730s Venice. Among the stucco decorations in yellow and green, we find details that echo the relief work on Cordova leather, very much in fashion in Venice in the eighteenth century.

The Empire room was redecorated for the visit of the Viceroy of Italy Eugene de Bauharnais in 1807. In the yellow room, we can admire a beautiful ceiling frescoed by Guarana, a student of Giambattista Tiepolo, rediscovered during the recent restoration directed by Toto Bergamo Rossi, director of the international foundation Venetian Heritage, whose mission is the preservation, restoration, and promotion of Venetian artistic heritage.

Other areas feature frescoes by Giovanni Carlo Bevilacqua and David Rossi.

What remains today of the Gradenigo gardens, restored in 2001, is about one-fourth the size of the original. Between the two world wars, part of the palace was sold and divided up into apartments, and part of the park was confiscated by the Fascist government to build housing for railway workers.

Today, a pergola covered by white wisteria, regularly pruned in topiary style, adorns the background of the garden. On the opposite side, toward the canal, we find another pergola covered by vines. In the center, shaped like a fountain, is a Japanese pagoda tree from the 1920s. Two long flowerbeds run alongside the walls of the palace and the garden, delimiting the gravel paths surrounding the central lawn. The English-style flowerbeds are designed by the homeowner and host a variety of aromatic perennial plants, typical of Venetian gardens, which flower from May to October. The central lawn has a simple rectangular shape with the corners rounded off in quarter-circles, echoing a traditional motif in Venetian flooring.

BELOW: In the entrance of the apartment, a few ancient stools serve as shelves for books and mail. In the background, a great eighteenth-century tapestry in red velvet with an embroidered lion of Saint Mark, the symbol of the Venetian Republic, at the center.

RIGHT (TOP): The French doors at the end of the stairway lead directly to the garden. In front of the doors, the pavement is decorated with precious geometrical designs in red Verona marble, black Belgian marble, and white Carrara marble. (BOTTOM): In a shaded corner of the garden we see varieties of Hydrangea, such as the *Hydrangea quercifolia*. The back wall is covered by evergreen star jasmine (*Trachelospermum jasminoides*).

OPPOSITE: The corridor of the entrance is decorated with stucco and eighteenth-century *grisaille* stuccoes. The great archive cabinet with a metal screen houses the owner's precious art books. The walnut doors are from the early eighteenth century.

PREVIOUS SPREAD: The *sala gialla*, or yellow room, is also called *salone del Guarana*, after the artist who painted the great fresco on the ceiling. It is adorned with Venetian furniture from the eighteenth century and the neoclassical period. On the Empire console table is a bust of Hebe by Antonio Canova, and above the wooden column is a portrait of a Venetian admiral by Alessandro Vittoria. On the walls in the background, a great eighteenth-century coat of arms of the Pesaro family is painted on wood, taken from a Venetian galley.

OPPOSITE: Recent restoration work in this room has brought to light the beautiful fresco decorations on the ceiling made by David Rossi in 1807 for the visit of the Viceroy of Italy Eugène de Beauharnais. The Venetian armchairs and mirror are from the Louis XVI period, while the table, the *gueridon*, and the bed, used as a sofa, are neoclassical. The late eighteenth-century chandelier is from Genoa and perfectly matches the decorations of the ceiling.

LEFT (TOP): In the *salone del Guarana* is an Empire walnut console and mirror. Four prints by Piranesi decorate one of the yellow marbled plaster walls. (BOTTOM): A nineteenth-century print of the Palazzo Gradenigo on Rio Marin.

ABOVE: A Venetian lantern from an eighteenth-century ship.

GAMBERI AL LIMONE

Prawns in Lemon-Herb Sauce

SERVES 4
· 1 clove garlic
· 3 sprigs flat-leaf parsley
· 3 sprigs dill
· Juice of 2 lemons
· ¾ cup (200 ml) extra virgin olive oil
· 1¼ lb. (600 g) prawns

Make the sauce: Finely chop the garlic, parsley, and dill. Combine the lemon juice with the olive oil, chopped garlic, and herbs.

Shell the prawns. Bring 4 cups (1 liter) of water to a boil and throw in the prawns. Simmer for 5 minutes, then drain. Drizzle with the sauce and serve.

ORATA ALLA GRIGLIA

Grilled Sea Bream

SERVES 4
· 2 oz. (50 g) flat-leaf parsley
· 1⅔ cups (3½ oz. / 100 g) fresh breadcrumbs or 1 scant cup (3½ oz. / 100 g) packaged breadcrumbs
· 1 clove garlic
· 3 tablespoons extra virgin olive oil
· 1 sea bream, cleaned and gutted
· 4 *datteri* tomatoes (small plum tomatoes)

Preheat the oven to 350°F (180°C).

Make a pesto: Chop the parsley, and, using a pestle and mortar, grind it with the breadcrumbs, garlic, and olive oil to make a paste.

Fill the cavity of the sea bream with the paste.

Place in an ovenproof dish and dot the tomatoes around. Cover with foil so that the fish does not dry out and cook for 20 to 25 minutes, depending on the size of the fish.

Serve with slices of polenta (see recipes on pages 68 and 124).

OPPOSITE: The table is set with glasses of blown Murano glass from the 1950s, neoclassical porcelain dishes, and a linen tablecloth made by Stella Cattana.

SARDE IN SAOR

Sweet and Sour Sardines

SERVES 4

· 2 lb. (1 kg) fresh sardines
· 2 tablespoons flour
· 3¼ cups (800 ml) extra virgin olive oil, divided
· 1 lb. (500 g) sweet onions
· 3 tablespoons white wine vinegar
· Salt and freshly ground pepper

A day ahead: Prepare the sardines by removing the central bone and head. Dip each one in the flour to coat.

In a skillet, heat 2½ cups (600 ml) of the olive oil, and, working in batches, deep fry the sardines for about 5 minutes. When they are cooked through, place them on sheets of paper towels to drain.

Finely slice the onions. In another skillet, heat the remaining oil and sauté the onions for 10 minutes, until pale. Stir in the vinegar and season with salt and pepper. Reduce the heat to low, and cook for another few minutes, until the sauce is thick.

In a terrine, arrange a layer of sardines. Cover with a layer of onion sauce. Repeat the procedure, finishing with a layer of onion sauce. Cover and marinate for 10 hours in the refrigerator.

RIGHT (TOP): A detail of the entrance to the ground floor, with a typical bench used in the Venetian *androne* and the family coat of arms painted on wood. (BOTTOM): On the walls of the dining room, an assortment of stucco decorations, dated around 1730, and en *grisaille* frescoes.

POLENTA ALLA GRIGLIA

Grilled Polenta Slices

SERVES 4

· 2 lb. (1 kg) cornmeal for polenta
· 1 tablespoon (20 g) kosher salt

Following the instructions given for the recipe on page 124, prepare the polenta.

When it is cooked, spread it over a dampened cutting board and allow it to cool. When cold, cut it into slices. Heat a cast-iron griddle pan and when hot, grill the slices so that the marks are visible on both sides.

INSALATA DI MARE

Seafood Salad

SERVES 6

· 5 oz. (150 g) small octopus
· 5 oz. (150 g) shelled shrimp
· 5 oz. (150 g) shelled scampi (Norway lobster)
· 5 oz. (150 g) cuttlefish
· 1 bunch chervil
· ¼ cup (60 ml) extra virgin olive oil
· Juice of 1 lemon
· Salt and freshly ground pepper

Prepare the seafood: Bring a large pot of water to a boil and add the seafood. Drop in first the octopus, then the shrimp, and finally, the scampi, leaving each type for 2 to 3 minutes before removing them with a sieve. Set aside ¾ cup (200 ml) of the cooking liquid.

In a saucepan with a little olive oil and the reserved cooking liquid, sauté the cuttlefish for 15 minutes. Drain and allow to cool to lukewarm.

Make the sauce: Chop the chervil. Combine the olive oil, lemon juice, and chervil well. The flavors will act as a foil to the flavors of the seafood fumet.

Serve the seafood salad drizzled with the sauce.

LEFT: A small painting by Davide Battistin inspired by Ingres's *Source* rests on the music stand of the grand piano in the *salone del Guarana*.
OPPOSITE: On the console table in the dining room, a small glass carafe with the coat of arms of Bartolomeo Colleoni, an illustrious ancestor of the master of the house.

A patrician's residence

CA'ZEN AI FRARI

P alazzo Zen was built at the end of the fourteenth century by Carlo Zen—*capitano da mar*, or "sea captain"—the hero of the war of Chioggia, in which the Venetians defeated their Genoese rivals in 1380. The Zen family is ancient and since the time of the Partecipazio-Badoer has always played an important role in the city. Members of the family include Renier Zen, who became doge in 1253, as well as ambassadors, senators, and cardinals. The palace underwent several modifications over the centuries. The most important innovations were the work of the famous architect Antonio Gasparri, a student of Baldassare Longhena, who, in the early eighteenth century, redesigned the inner courtyard while keeping the fifteenth-century stairway, and also built a new wing. The beautiful facade of the palace overlooking the San Stin canal is still predominantly Gothic and is surmounted by two elegant eighteenth-century obelisks. In some of the rooms, we can still admire decorations from the early eighteenth century. One room in particular is adorned with stucco cherubs in full-relief by Abbondio Stazio.

A new decorating program was commissioned by Alessandro Zen, ambassador of Venice at the court of Louis XV in Versailles, during the course of which many of the rooms were frescoed and adorned with paintings by the great Venetian artists of the mid-eighteenth century, such as Antonio Pellegrini, Giacomo Guarana, and Jacopo Amigoni.

At the end of the eighteenth century, notwithstanding the fall of the Venetian Republic and the serious economic crisis, the Zen family continued to have work done on the palace, redecorating some rooms in the neoclassical style.

After more than six centuries, the Zen family still owns the palazzo, and Nicolò and Elena Frigerio Zeno continue to take good care of the building and their beautiful garden.

BELOW: Sumptuous stucco decorations adorn the walls and the ceiling of one of the rooms on the second floor.

TOP RIGHT AND OPPOSITE: The doors of the *enfilade* rooms are adorned above with stucco reliefs picturing mythological scenes and fresco portraits of illustrious ancestors.

BELOW RIGHT: In the entrance, an eighteenth-century wrought iron lantern, a typical entrance bench, and the coat of arms of the Zeno family, painted on wood.

PREVIOUS SPREAD: In the Hercules room, the floor, the steps to the French doors, and the shutters of the same are decorated with carvings of various types of wood. In the center, a portrait of a Zeno cardinal. BELOW: The *portego*, or grand salon of the Ca' Zen, was redecorated in the mid-nineteenth century with monochrome frescoes and large mirrors. OPPOSITE: A silver sauceboat holding tomato sauce accompanies traditional stuffed turnovers called *panzerotti*. The table is finely embroidered in imitation antique Cordova leather.

PANZEROTTI

Cheese Turnovers

SERVES 4

Dough:
· 2 cups (9 oz. / 250 g) all-purpose flour
· ⅓ oz. (10 g) fresh yeast
· A little salt

Cheese Filling:
· 3½ oz. (100 g) Fontina cheese
· Scant ½ cup (2 oz. / 50 g) ricotta
· ¼ cup (2 oz. / 50 g) grated Parmigiano Reggiano
· 1 egg, lightly beaten
· Oil for frying
· Salt and freshly ground pepper

Make the dough: Combine the flour and yeast with ¾ cup (200 ml) of lukewarm water. Knead until smooth and allow to rise for 2 hours.

Make the turnovers: Roll the dough out and cut it into 10 triangles.

Cut the Fontina cheese into small cubes. Combine the ricotta and grated Parmigiano, and then stir in the cubes of Fontina. Season with salt and pepper.

Drop a spoonful of the cheese mixture on each triangle of dough. Seal the triangles, moistening the edges with a little water so that they remain closed. Heat the oil until it is sizzling. Brush the turnovers with the egg, and fry the turnovers on each side until golden.

RISI E BISI

Risotto with Garden Peas

SERVES 4

· 2 lb. (1 kg) peas in their pods
· 1 spring onion
· 4 tablespoons (2 oz. / 60 g) butter, divided
· 2 oz. (50 g) cooked ham, finely diced
· ¾ cup (9 oz. / 250 g) round grain rice (vialone nano)
· ¾ cup (200 ml) Pinot Grigio
· 1 bunch flat-leaf parsley, chopped
· ⅓ cup (2 oz. / 60 g) Parmigiano Reggiano, grated
· Salt and freshly ground pepper

Shell the peas, reserving the pods. Bring 4¼ US pints (2 liters) of water to a boil and drop in the peapods. Cook them for about 30 minutes. Drain well, reserving the liquid to make the risotto.

Chop the spring onion. Melt half of the butter in a skillet, and sauté the onion with the diced ham. Stir in the rice, peas, and wine. Mix well. When the wine has evaporated, gradually pour in the cooking liquid from the pods, stirring regularly for about 15 minutes. (This makes a risotto that is al dente.) Just before the rice is cooked, stir in the diced ham.

Remove from the heat and stir in the chopped parsley. Stir in the remaining butter and grated Parmigiano. Season with salt and pepper, and serve immediately.

RISOTTO PRIMAVERA

Risotto with Spring Vegetables

SERVES 4

· 2 lb. (1 kg) peas in their pods, for 14 oz. (400 g) shelled peas
· 2 baby carrots
· 2 small zucchini (courgettes)
· 3 spring onions
· 4 cups (1 liter) chicken broth
· 3 tablespoons (2 oz. / 50 g) butter, divided
· 1½ cups (10 oz. / 300 g) round grain rice, preferably Vialone or Arborio
· Scant ½ cup (100 ml) white wine, such as Tocai del Piave
· ¾ cup (5 oz. / 150 g) Parmigiano Reggiano, grated

Shell the peas. Wash and peel the carrots and zucchini. Dice the vegetables finely. Peel and chop the onions.

Bring the chicken stock to a boil.

In a heavy-bottomed saucepan over medium-high heat, melt 1 tablespoon (20 g) of the butter, and sauté the onions and vegetables until golden. Throw in the rice and pour in the wine. Allow the wine to evaporate. Continue stirring for about 18 minutes, regularly adding hot chicken broth.

Remove the risotto from the heat, and stir in the remaining butter and grated cheese, combining the ingredients thoroughly. Cover with the lid, allow to rest for 2 minutes, then serve.

Variations: Instead of the vegetables listed here, you might want to try asparagus tips, spinach leaves, artichoke bottoms, or celery sticks.

SORBETTO DI ARANCE

Frosted Oranges

SERVES 4
· 4 oranges
· ¾ cup (200 ml) whipping cream
· ⅓ cup (2½ oz. / 75 g) sugar
· 1 egg

Cut the top off each orange and scoop out the flesh, taking care not to cut into the peel.

Process or blend the orange flesh with the cream, sugar, and egg until the mixture is smooth and creamy.

Fill each orange with this orange cream and freeze for 12 hours before serving.

TOP: A precious mercury mirror above a neoclassical console table.
LEFT: A large mirror adorns the back wall of the archive room. The console table dates to the eighteenth century. The walls are covered in silk *moirée* by Rubelli.

THE GARDENS OF GIUDECCA ISLAND

Giudecca Island, opposite St. Mark's, has for centuries been home to wonderful gardens, game pavilions, meeting places for idle nobles, and a refuge for Venetians escaping the heat of the city. The palazzi gardens, nestled behind high brick walls, are often an extension of water inlets. Lush wreaths of wisteria and star jasmine grow along posts made of weeping willow. Elegance is provided by rows of artfully sculpted boxwood trees, with a cypress-lined path leading to a music kiosk. In the eighteenth century, Venetians would play card games here (gambling was fashionable) or come to dance. Some nobles created veritable botanical gardens on the island, planting decorative flowers, aromatic herbs, and even a few rows of table grape vines. The Bauer Palladio Hotel & Spa (see facing page) has a vegetable patch that Francesca Bortolotto Possati has restored in the style of a fragrance garden.

The magnificent residence of an aristocratic pianist

CA' MOCENIGO

in San Samuele

The Mocenigo family settled in Venice around the year 1000. They were therefore one of the "new houses," distinguished from the founding families and those who were already in Venice before the seat of the Republic was moved to Rialto in the eighth century. Nevertheless, the Mocenigo is one of the three most illustrious and powerful families in the history of the Serenissima, boasting a great number of dogi, second only to that of the Contarini. At the end of the eighteenth century, there were no less than fifteen different branches of the family.

The famous Mocenigo palaces in the parish of San Samuele are composed of three different buildings that vary in dimension and style. The most ancient one, called Casa Vecchia, is of medieval origin but it was completely rebuilt by a student of Longhena toward the mid-seventeenth century. Palace Mocenigo, also called Casa Nuova or Nero, has two *piani nobili*, the first and second floors, adorned with Venetian windows and a facade entirely covered in Istrian stone. The style is late-sixteenth century.

Between these two palaces, there are two twin buildings of low height that have entrances, stairways, and independent courtyards in the late-sixteenth-century style. The facades were once decorated with frescoes that have since been lost. Lord Byron stayed in this palace, which is now the only one that still belongs, in part, to the Mocenigo descendents. In some of the rooms, important mementos of Venetian history are found, such as the ducal horn (headdress) of Doge Alvise Mocenigo I, and the trowel with which the same doge laid the first stone of the church of the Redentore alla Giudecca, built as an *ex voto* to celebrate the end of the pestilence, in 1577.

The marchesa Olga de Cadaval, great matron of the arts, friend of famous musicians, and daughter of the last Mocenigo of the San Samuele branch, received artists like Igor Stravinsky and his faithful friend Arthur Rubinstein, Mstislav Rostropovic, and many others in the palace. Today this ancient residence is inhabited by the pianist Don Enrique Perez de Guzman, who continues the musical tradition of the house, entertaining his hosts with concerts, played on a piano on which Rubinstein himself played more than once. In the palace, we can admire a great unfinished statue of Napoleon, sculpted in 1808 by Angelo Pizzi, a student of Canova. It had been commissioned by Alvise Mocenigo VI, and was originally meant to be placed in the garden of the Mocenigo country residence in Alvisopoli, in the Venetian countryside.

BELOW: Through the glass door, late eighteenth-century furniture.
RIGHT (TOP): A Steinway grand piano and a large painting of the family tree.
(BOTTOM): A photographic portrait of the great pianist Arturo Benedetti Michelangeli.
OPPOSITE: Beneath the portrait of the tenant's mother, pillows lined with precious velvet from the ancient manufactory of the Cavenezia brothers.

PREVIOUS SPREAD: The dining room is decorated with an imposing gilded and carved wooden frieze. A number of paintings from the Venetian school adorn the walls, which are covered with precious damask tapestries. The chandelier is made of Bohemia crystal. On the table, two English candelabrums of gilded bronze picturing mythological divinities.

ABOVE: In the entrance, above a Venetian walnut *banquette* of the mid-eighteenth century, a neoclassical mirror lacquered in white and gold.

OPPOSITE: The nineteenth-century walnut door is decorated with the Mocenigo coat of arms surmounted by the ducal horn.

Pears in Red Wine

SERVES 4

· 2 cups (500 ml) red wine
· 4 to 6 pears (we use pears from Sant'Erasmo)
· Scant ⅓ cup (2 oz. / 60 g) sugar
· A handful of walnuts

In a large pot, bring the red wine to a boil. Peel the pears and carefully place them in the boiling wine. Stir in the sugar. Cover with the lid, reduce the heat to low, and simmer gently for about 30 minutes, or until the pears are cooked. Check to see if they are done with the tip of a knife: they should not be hard, but must remain firm.

Serve the pears in bowls with the wine syrup and scatter with a few walnuts.

OPPOSITE: The *appliques*, the frames of the mirrors, and the consoles in the dining room are all of gilded and carved wood.
TOP RIGHT: On top of an ancient cupboard of walnut root, precious goblets of Murano glass.
PAGE 99: On a gilded wood console, a *semifreddo* of soft fruit is served in a Murano glass dish.

SEMIFREDDO AI FRUTTI DI BOSCO

Semifreddo with Berry Compote

SERVES 4

For the Semifreddo
· 3 eggs (you will have 1 egg white left over)
· ½ cup (3½ oz. / 100 g) sugar, divided
· 1 sachet vanilla sugar (or 1 teaspoon vanilla extract)
· 2 cups (500 ml) whipping cream, well chilled

For the Berry Compote
· 8 oz. (250 g) assorted berries: raspberries, blackberries, and red currants
· 1 tablespoon (20 g) butter
· 1½ tablespoons (20 g) sugar
· Scant ½ cup (100 ml) orange juice

Prepare the cream: Separate the eggs, reserving 1 egg white for another use. In a mixing bowl, whisk ⅓ cup (3 oz. / 80 g) of the sugar, the vanilla sugar, and the 3 egg yolks until frothy. In a clean mixing bowl, whisk the 2 egg whites until they hold firm peaks.

In another mixing bowl, whisk the cream with the remaining sugar until it holds soft peaks. Carefully fold the whipped egg whites into the whipped cream, then fold this mixture into the yolk-sugar mixture.

Line a 4 x 8-inch loaf pan with plastic wrap. Pour the semifreddo mixture into the pan and cover with more plastic wrap. Freeze for 5 hours.

Prepare the berry compote: Rinse the berries under running water. Melt the butter in a skillet with the sugar. Stir in the berries and orange juice and simmer over low heat for 5 minutes.

Fifteen minutes before serving, remove the semifreddo from the freezer and allow it to thaw slightly for 15 minutes. Serve slices of the semifreddo in dessert bowls and spoon the berry compote over the top.

GALANI DI CARNEVALE

Carnival Cookies

SERVES 4
· 2 cups (9 oz. / 250 g) flour
· 2 eggs
· 10 drops orange flower water
· 1 tablespoon sugar
· 1 pinch salt
· Finely grated zest of 1 lemon
· 2 tablespoons (25 g) butter, softened
· Oil for frying
· Confectioners' sugar for dusting

Pour the flour into a mixing bowl and make a well in the center. Using a fork, incorporate the eggs, orange flower water, sugar, salt, lemon zest, and butter. Knead together, then roll the dough out thinly and cut it into small diamond shapes, ½ inch x 1 inch (1 cm x 2 cm).

Heat the oil in a pot, and, working in batches if necessary, fry the diamonds on both sides. Drain on sheets of paper towels.

Dust with confectioners' sugar and serve.

SUGAR

La Serenissima asserted its power through trade and conquests thanks to its formidable armada. Venetian merchants discovered sugar in Cyprus—where *canna mielata*, or sugar cane, flourished—when they colonized the island. After the discovery of the Americas, Venice increased importations, and in 1652, two million pounds of sugar reached the maritime customs posts. The refinery was located in San Cassiano. It is said that, in 1574, when Henri III, King of France and Poland, visited the Arsenal to acquire galleys, Doge Alvise Mocenigo received him for a revelatory meal. There were surprises in store for the king: his napkin was made of sugar and the table was decorated with sugar figurines, triumphal arches, and miniature boats. The coats of arms of France and Poland were made of sugar; there were finely sculpted sugar statues of saints and of the guests. Subsequently, sugar production became a prerogative of Venice, where *confetti*–sugar-coated almonds–for weddings and christenings were produced.

At dinner with a lady from New Zealand

PALAZZETTO DUODO

in San Stae

A noble residence dating back to the thirteenth century, the palace was renovated by the mid-fifteenth century but maintained its proportions. The facade is Venetian Gothic and has a single *piano nobile*, or second floor, unlike other contemporary buildings which always had two. The four lights in the central window and in the lateral windows all end with pointed arches.

The name of the building comes from the ancient noble family of Duodo, documented since 1200 in the history of the Venetian Republic.

Mimi and John Todhunter have been living in this fascinating house for the last ten years, enjoying the original high wooden ceilings and the typical Venetian floors. Mimi uses the *portego* not only as an antechamber but also as a dining room. In one of the side rooms, she has set up a professional kitchen, from which delicious meals are served on beautiful porcelain and ceramics.

Dinner is served on splendidly decorated tables with linen napkins dating to the early 1900s. A collection of antique linen can also be found in a beautiful seventeenth-century wardrobe.

A small garden, decorated with statues and ancient stone elements, functions also as an entrance to the house from the ground floor.

BELOW: Detail of the stairs leading to the second floor.
RIGHT (TOP): The owner of the house keeps a unique collection of antique linens in a large seventeenth-century wardrobe.
OPPOSITE: Table laid for an informal brunch with dishes of Hungarian porcelain by Herend, Bohemia crystal cups, and silver cutlery. The linen tablecloth is by Stella Cattana.

RISOTTO ALLA ZUCCA

Pumpkin Risotto

SERVES 4

· 1¾ cup (14 oz. / 400 g) pumpkin flesh
· 2 sweet onions
· 3 tablespoons extra virgin olive oil, divided
· 2 cups (14 oz. / 400 g) round grain rice, preferably Vialone or Arborio
· ¾ cup (200 ml) white wine
· 6 cups (1½ liters) hot chicken broth
· 1 bunch flat-leaf parsley, chopped
· 5 tablespoons (80 g) butter
· ½ cup (3½ oz. / 100 g) Parmigiano Reggiano, grated

Cut the pumpkin flesh into small cubes.

Chop the onions and sauté them in 2 tablespoons of the olive oil. Add the rice and pour in the wine, allowing it to evaporate. Stir in the pumpkin cubes. Gradually pour in the chicken broth, adding more only once the previous addition has been absorbed. It is important for the preparation to retain a liquid consistency. Cook for 15 to 20 minutes, stirring regularly. Sprinkle with the parsley.

Remove from the heat and stir in the butter, ensuring that it is thoroughly combined.

For an attractive presentation, serve the risotto in a Bassano ceramic dish, or in a carefully hollowed-out pumpkin skin. Serve the grated Parmigiano on the side.

OPPOSITE: Pumpkin risotto is served in a Bassano pumpkin-shaped ceramic bowl. The antique linen napkins are embroidered with initials in relief.

ROMBO ALLA VENEZIANA

Venetian-Style Turbot

SERVES 4
· 1 fennel bulb
· 1 red onion
· One 2-lb. (1-kg) turbot
· 6 green olives
· 6 cherry tomatoes
· 1 sprig dill
· 3 tablespoons extra virgin olive oil
· Salt and freshly ground pepper

Preheat the oven to 320°F (160°C).

Cut the fennel bulb into quarters and the red onion into thin rounds.

Place the fish in an appropriately-sized ovenproof dish. Arrange the fennel quarters, onion rounds, olives, cherry tomatoes, and pieces of dill sprig around it. Drizzle with the olive oil and season with salt and pepper. Cover with a sheet of foil, and cook for 40 minutes.

TOP: Nineteenth-century silver cutlery.
BOTTOM: A detail of the *portego* with two round *habillé* tables.

CREMA DI KIWI AI FRUTTI DI BOSCO

Kiwi Purée with Red Berries

SERVES 4

· 3 kiwis
· Scant ⅔ cup (4 oz. / 120 g) sugar
· 1 cup (4 oz. / 125 g) raspberries
· 1 cup (4 oz. / 125 g) red currants

Crush or purée the kiwis with the sugar. Divide the purée among four dessert bowls. Arrange the raspberries and red currants over the purée.

Serve the fruit with traditional Venetian cornmeal *zaletti* cookies (see recipe opposite) or *amaretti di Sarrano* (almond macaroons).

ZALETI

Biscotti di Farina di Polenta Venetian Cornmeal Cookies

SERVES 4 OR MAKES ABOUT 2 LB. (1 KG) COOKIES

· ⅔ cup (3½ oz. / 100 g) raisins
· 4 eggs
· ¾ cup (5 oz. /150 g) sugar
· 1½ cups (9 oz. / 250 g) cornmeal
· 2 cups (9 oz. / 250 g) all-purpose flour
· 1 pinch salt
· Seeds of 1 vanilla bean
· Finely grated zest of 1 unwaxed lemon
· 1¾ sticks (200 g) butter, softened
· A little milk (if necessary)
· Confectioners' sugar for dusting (optional)

Preheat the oven to 350°F (180°C).

Soak the raisins in a bowl of lukewarm water.

In a mixing bowl, whisk the eggs and sugar together.

In another mixing bowl, combine the cornmeal, flour, salt, vanilla seeds, and lemon zest. Drain the raisins. When the dry ingredients are thoroughly mixed, beat in the egg-sugar mixture, butter, and raisins. If the dough seems a little dry, add just enough milk to ensure that it is not too dense.

Shape the dough into small balls, and bake for 12 to 15 minutes, until lightly golden. Allow to cool on a rack, and then dust with confectioners' sugar if you wish.

OPPOSITE: Tea set in Herend porcelain and a Bassano ceramic fruit bowl. The furniture is from the eighteenth century.

A historical residence of artists

PALAZZETTO CONTARINI QUERINI

on Rio di San Polo

PAGE 114: From the bedroom of the palazzetto Contarini Querini, a small terrace overlooks Rio di San Polo.
OPPOSITE: In the atelier of Giovanni Soccol, a large linen sail can be raised with an ingenious system of ropes, allowing the artist to filter the light that floods the room through the large glass windows.

P alazzetto Contarini Querini is a fifteenth-century building overlooking Rio di San Polo, at the crossroads of a labyrinth of narrow winding canals in the heart of Venice. The small palace is known for having been the residence of artists since the early 1900s.

Emma Ciardi, painter and daughter of the famous painter Guglielmo Ciardi, settled on the last floor of the building, transforming it into an atelier and completely redecorating it according to her professional requirements and the taste of the time.

The result was a marvelous and singular space, with two great halls with large windows on the ceiling and the walls, resembling a painter's atelier in nineteenth-century Paris.

In the 1950s, the writer Pier Maria Pasinetti, nephew of Emma Ciardi, inherited the atelier where he wrote some of his novels, including *Rosso Veneziano*.

Since 1972, the house has been the residence of Venetian painter and architect Giovanni Soccol, who has managed to fully preserve the artistic atmosphere of the place.

The salon is adorned with Renaissance furniture and paintings. On the walls there are also works by the owner and by Gennaro Favai.

The atelier is a magical place: among Soccol's large canvases and small sketches that tell us of oneiric visions of labyrinths, constellations, and clouds. Like in a cabinet of curiousity, we see a great number of unusual items, such as the skull of one of Napoleon's horses, which he rode during the campaign of Italy and which died in Verona, placed above the entrance to the hall.

The kitchen is a lively and bustling part of the house, and serves also as a passage between the salon and the corridor leading to the guest rooms.

Giovanni Soccol and Magherita Tirelli are fond of entertaining their friends in this unusual residence. The glasses are made of antique Murano glass, each one different from the other. The eighteenth-century ceramic dishes are from the Venetian manufactories of Bassano and Este. Soccol embodies the tradition of Venetian "materica" art, achieving an effect by painting layers of thick color directly on the canvas.

BELOW: A view of the *altana*, the traditional Venetian wood terrace, positioned above the roof of palaces.
OPPOSITE: Giovanni Soccol always makes some preparatory sketches (hanging on the easel) before painting his large canvases.

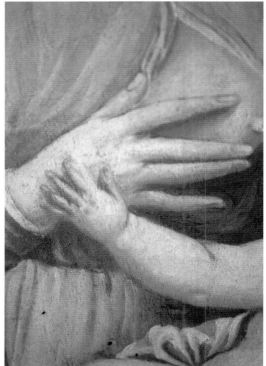

OPPOSITE: The artist in his study surrounded by books and family souvenirs. Covering a gilded wooden candelabrum, in the form of a large candle, is a lampshade of parchment designed by the homeowner. On the wall, a carved wooden angel and a large painting of the Venetian school both dating to the sixteenth century.
ABOVE: The entrance to the kitchen, an essential part of the house for Giovanni Soccol, who loves food and cooking.
FOLLOWING SPREAD: View of the San Polo district. In the background, the Basilica dei Frari.

POLENTA

Polenta (Basic Method)

SERVES 6

· 2 lb. (1 kg) classic polenta
· 1 tablespoon (20 g) kosher salt
· A little flour if necessary

Bring 6⅓ US pints (3 liters) of water to a boil with the kosher salt. Have another pot of boiling water ready in case the polenta thickens too much as it cooks.

Pour in two-thirds of the polenta, whisking constantly from the bottom of the pot to the surface, to prevent any lumps from forming. Continue whisking for 15 minutes, then pour in the remaining polenta. Cook for an additional 40 minutes, stirring regularly with the whisk. Add a little hot water if necessary, or a little flour if the mixture seems too thin.

The final consistency depends on what you are planning to make. If you will be frying slices or putting it in the oven to make a gratin, it should be fairly firm. To garnish a dish that has sauce, it should be fairly soft but must be served very hot. Keep in mind that there are several types of grains, from coarse to finely ground.

Polenta au Gratin
Oven-Baked Polenta

· Cooked polenta
· Various types of cheese, grated
· Parmigiano Reggiano, grated

Following the instructions above, cook the polenta. After about 25 minutes' cooking, stir in the grated cheese and continue cooking for another 30 minutes or so. Pour into an ovenproof dish and place under the broiler (or in a very hot oven), sprinkle with the grated Parmigiano, and bake for a few minutes.

BACCALÀ MANTECATO

Creamed Salted Cod

SERVES 4

· 2 lb. (1 kg) salted cod (Norwegian stockfish)
· 4 cups (1 liter) milk
· 2 cloves garlic
· ¾ cup (200 ml) extra virgin olive oil (select one with a mild flavor, rather than a fruity olive oil)
· Salt and freshly ground pepper

A day ahead (at least): Soak the cod in a bowl of water, changing the water frequently to remove the excess salt.

The next day, place the cod in a saucepan with the milk and bring to a boil, skimming if necessary. Place the garlic cloves in the boiling milk for 2 minutes to blanch them, then remove the saucepan from the heat. Cover with the lid and allow to rest for 20 minutes.

Drain the cod and carefully remove all the skin and the bones.

Using a garlic press, crush the garlic cloves. Cut the fish into pieces and, using a food processor or a mortar and pestle, grind it to a coarse purée with the garlic.

Using a wooden spoon, beat the purée energetically, gradually drizzling the oil in, just as you would to make mayonnaise. Make sure that you always stir in the same direction. Continue until the mixture is soft, creamy, and white. Season with salt and pepper.

You can serve the creamed salted cod hot, with grilled slices of polenta or, when it has cooled and chilled, on small slices of bread.

OPPOSITE: Imported from Norway for centuries, the baccalà or stockfish is a classic Venetian dish.

POLENTA

The poor man's dish of Venetian cuisine, polenta first appeared in northern Italy in the sixteenth century when Fernando Columbus, the son of Christopher, introduced corn to the region. Corn yields are higher than those of wheat, and corn production soon prospered. Polenta, made from corn flour that requires slow, patient cooking, was a staple for country folk until the mid-1950s. However, it is not too humble to appear on the tables of the well-off, and it has earned the title of the emblematic dish of Venice. With its lovely yellow hue, the creamy food even holds a place in art history: in the seventeenth century, using masterly brush strokes, Pietro Longhi captured a scene of polenta preparation. Polenta also made its theater debut in 1743, when Carlo Goldoni wrote in *La Donna di Garbo* (The Fashionable Woman, Act I, Scene IX): "When the water begins to boil, I will take this ingredient, a beautiful golden dust called yellow flour, and little by little I shall melt it in the cauldron [...]. We will then gradually throw on top of it an abundant portion of fresh, yellow, and delicate butter, then the same quantity of a fat, yellow, and well grated cheese." Polenta is always allowed to cool except when it can be served as a milky soup. Slicing polenta is a fine art: with food-safe twine, it is cut into slices or squares. Either fried or au gratin in the oven, it is served as a side dish with most traditional Venetian dishes.

PANE DI TONNO

Tuna Loaf

SERVES 4
· 1 lb. (500 g) boiled potatoes
· 1 lb. (500 g) canned tuna
· 4 tablespoons breadcrumbs
· 4 tablespoons grated Parmigiano Reggiano
· 4 eggs

Flake the tuna into the bowl of a food processor. Add the other ingredients, and process until smooth.

Shape the mixture into a loaf on a large sheet of aluminum foil, close tightly to make *en papillote*. Place in boiling water for 30 minutes. Remove from the water, and carefully take the loaf out of the foil.

Serve in slices, accompanied by asparagus.

ASPARAGI ALLA VENEZIANA

Venetian-Style Asparagus

SERVES 4
· 2 lb. (1 kg) white asparagus (we use Bassano asparagus)
· 4 eggs
· ¾ cup (200 ml) wine vinegar
· ¾ cup (200 ml) extra virgin olive oil

Bring a large pot of water to a boil.

Trim the asparagus, cutting them at least 1¼ to 1½ inches (3 to 4 cm) from the base. Carefully peel them, stopping short of the tips. Place in the boiling water and cook for about 20 minutes, or until softened. Remove the asparagus from the water and place the eggs in to cook until hard boiled.

Peel the eggs and crush them with a fork. Whisk in the vinegar and olive oil to make a sauce.

Serve the asparagus with the sauce on the side.

OPPOSITE: The fabulous *horror vacui* in the kitchen of the master of the house.

VERDURE PRIMAVERILI

Braised Spring Vegetables

SERVES 4

· 1 lb. (500 g) small purple artichokes
· 1 lb. (500 g) green or purple asparagus
· 1 cup (8 oz. / 250 g) peas
· 1 cup (8 oz. / 250 g) fresh fava beans
· 1 onion
· 3 garlic cloves
· 1 bunch flat-leaf parsley
· Salt and freshly ground pepper
· Extra virgin olive oil for the pot

Wash the artichokes and remove the outer leaves. Wash the asparagus and break each one into several chunks, discarding the hard base. Shell the peas and fava beans.

Blanch the fava beans in boiling water, then drain and peel them. Peel and chop the onion and the garlic cloves. Wash and chop the parsley.

In a large pot, heat a little olive oil and sauté the garlic, onion, and vegetables. Pour in a little water, cover with the lid, and braise for about 20 minutes. Season with salt and pepper, and sprinkle with the chopped parsley.

BELOW: In a corner of the room, an ancient cupboard houses a precious collection of Murano glass.

PASTICCIO ALLA TREVIGIANA

Wild Hops Torte

SERVES 4

· 2 bunches wild hops, or wild asparagus (in pieces), or 14 oz. (400 g) Swiss chard, green parts only
· 2 tablespoons sunflower seed oil
· Scant ½ cup (100 ml) white wine
· 1 generous cup (7 oz. / 200 g) rice semolina
· 1 cup (7 oz. / 200 g) Parmigiano Reggiano, grated, divided
· 1 tablespoon flour
· 7 tablespoons (3½ oz. / 100 g) butter, softened
· Salt and freshly ground pepper

Preheat the oven to 320°F (160°C). Lightly butter or oil a 12-inch (30 cm) cake pan.

Wash the hops (or wild asparagus, or Swiss chard) and dry well. Heat the oil in a skillet and sauté for a few minutes. Pour over the wine and season with salt and pepper. Cook a little further, until most of the liquid has evaporated or been absorbed.

Combine the rice semolina, three-quarters of the grated Parmigiano, the flour, and butter. Working with your fingertips, add the vegetables, continuing until the mixture forms large clumps—the same texture you would make for a crumble.

Place the batter in the cake pan, and sprinkle with the remaining grated Parmigiano. Bake for 15 minutes, until the edges and top are nicely golden. Transfer to a rack and cool. This savory torte, known as a *pasticcio*, should be served warm.

LEFT (TOP): Giovanni Soccol is fond of arranging curious bric-a-brac; in this case a glass eye, a compass, and a mirror. (BOTTOM): A carafe in crystal of Bohemia and a French porcelain coffee cup.
OPPOSITE: A curious nineteenth-century spoon and an ancient pewter dish.

VIOLETTO DI S.ERASMO
N°

VEGETABLE GROWERS

The small vegetable producers of Sant'Erasmo are the pride and joy of Venice; they supply the majority of the markets of the Rialto, the Castello, and the Dorsoduro, the city's main neighborhoods. On display are arrays of early vegetables, fruit, and, more than anything else, leafy greens. Prominent among them is the unique purple *cicoria di Chioggia*, or radicchio. The vegetable that reigns supreme, however, is the *carciofo violetto*, the small violet artichoke of Sant'Erasmo, which grows until winter and resists the first frosts. On April 25, the feast day of Saint Mark, patron saint of the city, the first artichokes of the season, known as the *Castraure*, are cut back to ensure they bloom for a second crop in the fall. The *Castraure* can be eaten raw in salad, fried, or cooked as part of a risotto. Artichoke bottoms, served with cardoons, fennel, or squash, are also served as accompaniments to meat dishes.

A game preserve

LA VALLE
SAN LEONARDO

I t only takes a few minutes of navigation to leave behind the crowds of Saint Mark's square and reach the islands of the lagoon. Away from the *calli*, the narrow streets packed with tourists, you reach the estuary of the Brenta river, favored by Hemingway who stayed here on more than one occasion. Here, you enter into a lost paradise, where nature, history, and humanity have been living in harmony for centuries. Herons, elegant avocets, stilts, lapwings, kingfishers: an incredible variety of birds awaits you, varying with the season, along with feathered game, such as teals and wigeons in the nearby ponds.

Marco Giol is the owner of the Valle San Leonardo estate, which he inherited from his grandfather, Giovanni. He uses his skills and passion to keep the old traditions of these areas alive, making hunting and fishing the main economic activities of the estate.

Here, hunters still practice the traditional "barrel hunt" of the lagoon, which consists of waiting patiently for the wild geese at early dawn, hiding in a barrel half-immersed in water.

Fishing is also a rewarding activity in December or at Lent, when eels arrive to the lagoon in great numbers after a long trip and can be captured with eel baskets, called *cogolli* in the local dialect.

Back at the hunting lodge, the hunters gather around the *fogher*, a curious circular fireplace, to warm up after a day of hunting and show off their trophies while drinking a cup of tea or a glass of local wine. The building is rustic but beautiful and very welcoming. It is adorned with antique furniture, wood paneling, and flooring with magnificent ancient majolica tiles, all well-looked after by the owner's mother. Stuffed animals and antique prints provide the final touch to this place from another time. An abundance of traditional food is served on magnificent porcelain dishes, a perfect combination of conviviality, sophistication, and good food!

RIGHT (TOP) AND OPPOSITE: Behind the hunting cason is the typical fireplace chimney. The inside of the lodge, called the *fogher* (fire), is decorated with a boiserie of larch wood and a semicircular bench.
BELOW: The *vestiere*, or coatroom, of the gamekeeper.

ANTIPASTI ALLA BRACE

Fire-Roasted Antipasti

SERVES 4
· 4 tablespoons extra virgin olive oil
· 3 sprigs fresh thyme
· 8 small scallops in their shells
· 1 prepared eel
· Salt and freshly ground pepper

Combine the olive oil, salt, pepper, and thyme leaves to make a sauce.

Open the scallops and brush them well with the sauce, reserving some for the eel. Place them on a rack directly over the fire (or under the broiler). Cook for about 10 minutes.

To cook the eel, cut it into chunks, brush them well with the sauce, and cook for about 10 minutes in the same way as the scallops.

TOP LEFT: The gamekeeper prepares the traditional fish soup and grilled eel.
LEFT: A goose quill is used to grease the food.

SALSA VERDE

Green Sauce

· 1 bunch flat-leaf parsley
· 2 salted anchovies, rinsed
· 2 heads garlic
· 1⅔ cups (3½ oz. / 100 g) fresh white breadcrumbs
· ¾ cup (200 ml) red wine vinegar
· Scant ½ cup (100 ml) extra virgin olive oil
· Salt to taste

In a food processor or in a blender, combine all the ingredients, gradually drizzling in the olive oil until the sauce reaches a creamy texture.
The green sauce can be served with the Venetian-Style Pot-au-Feu (opposite).

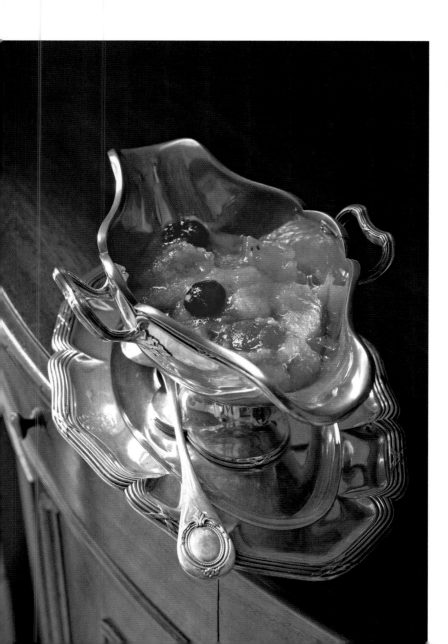

BOLLITO MISTO ALLA VENETA

Venetian-Style Pot-au-Feu

SERVES 4

· 6 carrots
· 3 onions studded with 2 cloves
· 3 stalks celery
· 3 bay leaves
· 1 bunch flat-leaf parsley
· 1 handful kosher salt
· 1 lb. (500 g) piece of whole veal shank
· 1 lb. (500 g) beef shoulder clod, or other piece
· 1 free-range chicken, or 1 capon
· 1 sausage for braising, such as *cotechino* (available from Italian specialty stores)

Wash and peel the vegetables. Divide the vegetables between three pots, each with about 8 cups (2 liters) salted, cold water.

Place the veal and beef in one pot, and the chicken and the sausage in a separate pot.

Cook the veal and beef for 1½ hours, the chicken for 1 hour, and the sausage for about 30 minutes. Prick the sausage with a fork or toothpick, wrap it in foil, and place in a pot of cold water. Bring to a gentle boil and cook for 30 to 45 minutes.

Drain the pieces of meat, the chicken, and the sausage, and cut each into slices or pieces. Serve hot, accompanied by small pickled white onions, gherkins, Cremona mustard, and Green Sauce (opposite).

LEFT AND OPPOSITE: Silver sauceboat with Cremona mustard. Venetian mixed boiled meat and *salsa verde* are served on porcelain dishes of Meissen.

ANATRA IN CASSERUOLA

Duck Casserole

SERVES 4

- 1 duck weighing 3 lb. (1½ kg) or 1 duck with the liver
- 1 garlic clove
- 1 sprig rosemary
- 2 sage leaves
- 3½ oz. (100 g) minced pork
- ¾ cup fresh or ½ cup packaged (2 oz. / 50 g) breadcrumbs
- Scant ½ cup (100 ml) milk
- ¼ cup (2 oz. / 50 g) Parmigiano Reggiano, grated
- 1 egg
- A little freshly grated nutmeg
- Salt and freshly grated pepper
- 3 tablespoons (50 g) butter, diced and softened, divided
- 3½ oz. (100 g) bacon, sliced
- ¾ cup (200 ml) white wine
- 2 slices Venetian *soppressa* (large, soft salami)

Preheat the oven to 430°F (220°C).

Mince together the liver, garlic, rosemary, and sage leaves, and combine with the minced pork.

Mix in the breadcrumbs, milk, grated cheese, egg, and a little freshly grated nutmeg. Season with salt and pepper. Mix in just enough butter to bind all the ingredients (1 to 2 tablespoons). Fill the cavity of the duckling with the stuffing and lace it up. Wrap the bacon slices around the duck. Melt the remaining butter in a pot and brown the bird on all sides.

Place in the oven. After 20 minutes of cooking, turn the duck and pour in the white wine. Cook for 1 hour 45 minutes, basting several times with the cooking juices.

Carve the duck and arrange the pieces on a serving platter.

TAGLIATELLE AL RAGÙ DI ANATRA

Tagliatelle with Duck Ragout

SERVES 4

- Leftovers from the duck casserole
- 1 14-oz. (400 g) can peeled tomatoes, with the juice
- ¾ cup (200 ml) red wine
- ½ lb. (250 g) egg tagliatelle
- ¼ cup (2 oz. / 50 g) Parmigiano Reggiano, grated
- Salt

Cut the leftover duck into pieces, and heat them in a skillet with the tomatoes and juice over medium-high heat. Stir in the red wine. Reduce the heat to low, and simmer until the sauce has reduced.

Cook the tagliatelle in a large pot of salted water. Drain the pasta, setting aside a little of the cooking liquid. Stir this liquid into the ragout sauce.

Serve the tagliatelle as soon as they are cooked, accompanied by the ragout sauce, and sprinkle with the grated Parmigiano.

RISOTTO AI FRUTTI DI MARE

Seafood Risotto

SERVES 4

· 1 lb. (500 g) mussels
· 1 lb. (500 g) wedge shells, (*telline*, which are very small clams), cockles, and clams, or an assortment of mollusks
· 4 cups (1 liter) fish fumet
· 1 lb. (500 g) shrimps
· 3 tablespoons olive oil, divided
· 2 shallots
· 1 garlic clove
· 2 cups (14 oz. / 400 g) round grain rice, preferably Vialone or Arborio
· Scant ½ cup (100 ml) white wine
· 1 bunch flat-leaf parsley, chopped
· 3 tablespoons (50 g) butter
· Salt and freshly ground pepper

Carefully wash the mollusks and shrimp. Place the mollusks in a large pot over high heat with a little oil until they have all opened. Shell them, leaving a few in their shells for decoration. Strain the cooking liquid and add it to the fish fumet. Place the shelled mollusks in a pot and cover with the lid.

Shell the shrimp, then sauté them with 1 tablespoon of the olive oil in a skillet over medium heat for 4 to 5 minutes. Cover with a lid and set aside.

In another pot, heat the fish fumet. Chop the shallots and garlic clove.

In a heavy-bottomed pot with the remaining oil, sauté the shallots and garlic for 3 minutes. Pour in the rice and sauté for 1 minute; do not allow the rice to color. Pour in the white wine and cook until evaporated.

Continue cooking the rice, gradually adding the hot fish fumet. Only add more fumet once the rice has absorbed the previous quantity. Cook for 15 to 20 minutes, stirring regularly. Stir in the shrimp, shelled mollusks, and 2 tablespoons of the chopped parsley, and cook for an additional 5 minutes (total cooking time should be 15 to 20 minutes). Season with salt and pepper.

Remove from the heat and stir in the butter. Garnish with the mollusks in their shells and sprinkle with the remaining chopped parsley. Cover with the lid and allow to rest for a few minutes before serving.

OPPOSITE: A canal in the valley with eel nets.
RIGHT: Detail of the entrance hall of the hunting mansion with a typical bench.

Dried Plum Cake

SERVES 6
- 2 oz. (50 g) prunes
- ¾ cup (200 ml) Marsala, or other fortified wine
- 1¼ cups (9 oz. / 250 g) sugar
- 4 eggs
- 2 sticks (9 oz. / 250 g) butter, melted and cooled, plus a little extra for the pan
- 2 cups (9 oz. / 250 g) flour, plus a little extra for the pan
- 1 scant tablespoon (11 g) baking powder
- Confectioners' sugar for dusting

A day ahead: soak the prunes in the Marsala.

To make the cake: Preheat the oven to 350°F (180°C). Butter a 16-inch (40 cm) cake pan and dust it lightly with flour.

Whisk the sugar and eggs together. Stir in the melted butter and then all of the flour and the baking powder. Mix until just combined. Drain the prunes.

Pour the batter into the prepared cake pan, dot the prunes around evenly, and bake for 30 minutes, until a cake tester inserted into the center comes out dry. Turn out of the pan and allow to cool.

Just before serving, dust generously with confectioners' sugar.

LEFT (TOP): A fishing hut with the traditional square fishing net. (BELOW): The dining room is decorated with nice *boiseries*. The floor and ceiling are made of larch wood.

FISHING AND HUNTING

The area around the Venetian lagoon is a land of both sea and fresh water, providing an ideal ecosystem for an extraordinarily varied range of both birds and fish. To preserve the equilibrium, hunting and fishing must be regulated. As early as the era of the doges, hawk hunting was reserved for the diplomatic visits of the Sultan of the Ottoman Empire. In the Middle Ages, fishing, as well as the means of fishing and the amount caught, were also subject to regulations established by the Most Serene Republic of Venice. Today, for more ecologically oriented reasons, hunting is reserved for private property owners, and only fishermen from the Chioggio Island are allowed to fish in the Adriatic Sea; their boats can throw anchor for a few hours to then sell their catch at the Rialto. Customers still hurry beneath the vaults of the fish market there to buy the catch of the day, including the famous *moleche*, small soft-shelled crabs from the lagoon.

A fifteenth-century villa among vineyards and gardens

CASA BASLINI

on the island of Torcello

The lagoon in Venice is an important ecosystem, the remnant of the enormous estuary that in Roman times extended from the north of Ravenna to Trieste. Marine fauna includes many species of fish, and there is also an abundance of sea birds, from seagulls, to stilts, to herons. There are only twenty-four people now living on Torcello, but the island once hosted as many as sixty thousand. The town was built by people who had come from the mainland to escape the barbarian invasions of the eighth, ninth, and tenth centuries. It then gradually lost its population when people began moving farther south to the islets of the archipelago, where Venice was eventually founded. On the island, we can still admire the cathedral of Santa Maria Assunta, famous for its beautiful mosaics; the Church of Santa Fosca; and the belltower—the symbol of the island—all in perfect condition.

In the small center of Torcello, we find the historical Locanda Cipriani, the inn favored by Ernest Hemingway, who would stay here when he went hunting in the nearby valleys and where he set his novel *Across the River, Beyond the Trees*. Today, Torcello is an oasis of peace and quiet in which you can immerse yourself in an uncontaminated natural environment, its beauty and intrigue compounded by the ancient churches and archaeological remains.

Casa Baslini is situated on the island of San Giovanni, connected to Torcello by a small bridge. It is the only building on the island that has remained intact and it was once part of the ancient religious complex of San Giovanni Evangelista, built before the year 1000, in whose Basilica (whose ruins are in the garden) the remains of Saint Barbara were preserved. The remains were later transferred to a convent, which was demolished during the Napoleonic period.

The house, a small Gothic palace dating to 1400, served as guest quarters for the convent. It later became the residence of fishermen and peasants until the 1950s, when it was restored along with the large garden, taking on its present appearance. In the garden, an archaeological excavation has brought to light the ancient church, whose remains are visible among the vines, the high cypress trees, and the delightful vegetable garden.

The Baslini family takes good care of this paradise of art and culture.

Guests are seduced by their light white wine, produced with grapes from the garden, and their excellent traditional lagoon cuisine, in which the vegetables from the garden also play a starring role.

BELOW: On the wall of the small dining room, a collection of German porcelain.
RIGHT (BOTTOM): A drawing from the house of Saxony was very fashionable on Venetian tables in the eighteenth century.
OPPOSITE: A corridor leads to the living room with portraits of the family.
FOLLOWING SPREAD: A delivery of vegetables arrives from a friend of the gardener's in a small boat.

CANESTRELLI OLIO E LIMONE

Baked Bay Scallops

SERVES 4
· 12 bay scallops or 4 scallops
· 1 garlic clove
· 1 bunch flat-leaf parsley
· 1 teaspoon breadcrumbs
· A little extra virgin olive oil

Preheat the oven to 320°F (160°C).

Open the scallops using a sharp knife and rinse them well.

Chop the garlic and parsley. Sprinkle the garlic and breadcrumbs over the scallops, and drizzle with a little olive oil. Bake for 10 minutes, scatter the chopped parsley on top, and serve them as an appetizer.

FIORI DI ZUCCA E ERBE FRITTE

Zucchini Blossom and Herb Fritters

SERVES 4
Batter for frying
· 1 egg
· ¾ cup plus 2 tablespoons (3½ oz. / 100 g) all-purpose flour
· ¾ cup (200 ml) milk

For the fritters
· 12 zucchini blossoms
· Sage leaves
· Rosemary leaves
· Oil for frying
· Salt

Make the batter: Separate the egg. In a mixing bowl, beat the yolk with the flour and milk until thoroughly combined. Whisk the egg white and fold it into the yolk, milk, and flour mixture.

Make the fritters: Pour the oil into a large frying pan (it should be sufficiently deep to at least half-cover the blossoms) and heat until it sizzles.

Dip the blossoms into the batter, and, working in batches if necessary, carefully place them in the oil. Turn them two or three times, until they are golden all over.

Remove with a slotted spoon and place on sheets of paper towels to drain. Fry the herbs using the same method. Season with salt and serve immediately.

FOLLOWING PAGES: The zucchini blossoms from the vegetable garden are a specialty of Villa Baslini. In the 1960s-style kitchen, utensils are placed in sight.

PASTA E FAGIOLI ALLA VENETA

Pasta with Borlotti Beans

SERVES 4

· 1 garlic clove
· 1 onion
· 1 stalk celery
· 1½ cups (400 ml) extra virgin olive oil, divided
· 3½ oz. (100 g) piece of bacon
· 10 oz. (300 g) fresh, shelled borlotti (cranberry) beans, or the same weight in dried white beans, soaked overnight in cold water
· 7 oz. (200 g) fresh tagliatelle
· ¾ cup (5 oz. / 150 g) Parmigiano Reggiano, grated
· 4 tablespoons fine-quality olive oil for serving
· Salt and freshly ground pepper

Chop the garlic, onion, and celery stalk. Pour 2 tablespoons of the olive oil into a large pot and lightly sauté the chopped vegetables; they should color only very lightly. Add the piece of bacon and the beans, and pour in 5¼ US pints (2½ liters) of water. Bring to a boil and cook for 1 hour 15 minutes. Remove the bacon, season with salt and pepper, and cook for an additional 1 hour 15 minutes.

Slice the bacon into matchstick slices (you can place them on the table for guests to help themselves).

Process half of the cooked beans until smooth. Return the puréed beans to the pot, and bring back to a boil. Cook the tagliatelle in the borlotti bean soup for about 15 minutes, tasting for doneness.

Serve in soup bowls, top with the grated cheese, and spoon 1 tablespoon of the oil on top. Accompany with a red Tocai wine (we like Tocai Rosso dei Colli Berici).

RISOTTO ALLE FRAGOLE

Strawberry Risotto

SERVES 4

For 4 cups (1 liter) chicken broth:
· 1 carrot
· 1 celery stalk
· 1 onion, studded with 1 clove
· 1 chicken wing or 1 piece beef short plate

For the risotto:

· 5 oz. (150 g) ripe strawberries
· 1 onion
· 3 tablespoons (50 g) butter, divided
· 2½ cups (1 lb. / 500 g) round-grain rice, such as Vialone or Arborio
· ¾ cup (200 ml) dry white wine
· Salt and freshly ground pepper

Make the chicken broth ahead of time: Bring 4 cups (1 liter) of water to a boil with the vegetables and chicken wing or beef. As the liquid heats up, skim to remove the foam from the surface. Allow to simmer at low heat for 1 hour 15 minutes. Using a slotted spoon, remove the vegetables and meat. The broth is now ready to use.

Make the risotto: Wash and hull the strawberries, and cut them into quarters. Chop the onion and sauté it very lightly in half of the butter; it should not brown. Pour in the rice and stir for 2 minutes, until the grains are translucent. Pour in the white wine and allow it to evaporate. Gradually add the hot broth, stirring constantly, adding more broth only when the rice has absorbed the liquid in the pan. After 10 to 15 minutes, stir in the strawberry quarters.

Remove from the heat, and stir in the remaining butter. Season with salt and pepper, mix well, and serve immediately.

VINEYARDS

Very early on, various religious congregations settled on the islands of the lagoon, which is ideal for meditation and prayer. In Torcello, Santo Spirito, San Francesco des Desert, and Sant'Erasmo, convents, churches, chapels, and monasteries proliferated, and vines were introduced to make wine to celebrate Eucharist. The communities planted double rows of vines that grew and flourished, forming arbors for easy picking of the grapes—Fruili, Cabernet, Muscat, and Mezermino, all for white wines that would not stain the intricate Burano lacework covering the altars of the most beautiful churches. The Austrian occupation during the Third Italian War of Independence almost put an end to grape production, and it was only after the war that grapes were once again cultivated on the islands. Today, determined winemakers are working hard to restore prestige to these white wines. One such producer is Silvano Follador, who produces 100,000 bottles of a highly sought-after Prosecco.

A delightful neoclassical residence

VILLA CITTADELLA

in Saonara, Padua

On the outskirts of Saonara, a small town in the valley of Padua, rises the complex known as Villa Cittadella Vigodarzere (now Valmarana), a country residence designed entirely by architect Giuseppe Jappelli in 1816. His first clients were Cavalier Antonio Vigodarzere (1766-1835), followed by his nephew and adopted son Andrea Cittadella (1804-1870). Antonio Vigodarzere decided to set aside almost 13 hectares (32 acres) of his estate in Saonara as a park, where he planted more than 35,000 trees to surround and adorn his mansion, as well as to provide work for the town inhabitants, who at the time were suffering from a famine. Jappelli organized the gardens as a large, central quadrangular area, surrounded by moats, in which the northwest sector, behind the *barchessa* (the traditional Venetian rural building) served as a vegetable garden and orchard.

The estate can be accessed through two entrances on the sides of the temple. The one on the left leads to the rustic courtyard; the one on the right takes you to a path leading to the great elliptical lawn in front of the mansion. This area of the garden is enlivened by a wooded hill and by gentle undulations of the ground, among which remnants of columns and statues can be seen, simulating classical ruins.

To the north, the rippling of the earth becomes more pronounced and in the woods one can see the rocky mouth of a tunnel leading to a jagged pond. The villa's interiors still retain the original French furniture designed by Jappelli, modeled after the fashionable French items designed by Fontaine and Percier for Josephine Bonaparte's Malmaison chateau.

Saonara now belongs to Count Lodovico Valmarana, who inherited it from the Cittadella Vigodarzere family. Over the years, he has admirably directed the restoration of the garden and villa. His wife, Barbara, president of the Foundation Amici della Fenice di Venezia, often hosts guests in the magnificent dining room, decorated completely in the Empire style. Her cakes are memorable, based on homemade recipes that remain today an impenetrable secret.

Saonara now belongs to count Lodovico Valmarana, who inherited it from the Cittadella Vigodarzere family. Over the years, count Valmarana has admirably directed the restoration of the garden and villa. His wife Barbara, president of the Foundation Amici della Fenice di Venezia, often hosts guests in the magnificent dining room, completely decorated in Empire style. Her cakes are memorable, based on house recipes that remain today an impregnable secret.

BELOW: In the park, inside a large architectural niche, a sculpted mask at the base of the statue serves as a fountain.
RIGHT (TOP): To the left of the kitchen service hatch, a slicing machine.
RIGHT (BOTTOM): Detail of the dining room, with service hatch, shelf, and walnut chairs designed by Jappelli.
OPPOSITE: A little neoclassical salon, unaltered by the centuries, serves as passage to the dining room.

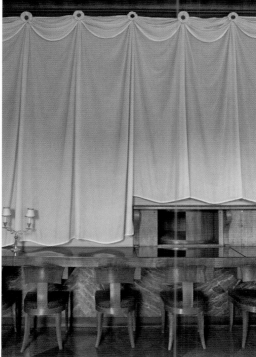

LEFT: The dining room was entirely designed by Jappelli, who drew inspiration from the French architects Fontaine and Percier and their decorations for the salon at Malmaison, the famous residence of Empress Josephine Bonaparte.

SCALOPPINE AL LIMONE E CARCIOFI

Veal Scaloppini with Artichoke Bottoms

SERVES 4

· 2 cloves garlic
· ¼ cup (60 ml) extra virgin olive oil, divided
· 8 artichoke bottoms
· Juice of 1 lemon
· 10 sprigs chives
· 1 tablespoon (20 g) butter
· 4 veal scaloppini
· 1 tablespoon flour
· ¾ cup (200 ml) white wine
· 1 lemon
· 4 sage leaves
· Salt and freshly ground pepper

Prepare the artichokes: Chop the garlic cloves and sauté in olive oil. Cut the artichoke bottoms into quarters and add them to the skillet. Season with salt and pepper, and drizzle with a few drops of the lemon juice. Allow to simmer over medium heat for 15 minutes, adding a little water if necessary. Chop the chives and sprinkle over the artichoke pieces. Keep warm.

Prepare the scaloppini: Melt the butter in a skillet or grill pan over medium heat. Cook the scaloppini on both sides for about 5 minutes altogether. Increase the heat to high, and pour in the white wine. Cover with a lid and braise the meat for 5 minutes. Remove the scaloppini from the skillet and keep warm. Deglaze the juices with the remaining lemon juice, stirring the flour into the juices until completely smooth.

Serve the scaloppini with the juices from the skillet, accompanied with the artichoke bottoms.

INSALATA DI FAGIOLI, GAMBERETTI E RUCOLA

White Bean and Shrimp Salad with Arugula

SERVES 4

· 1 lb. (500 g) dry white beans
· 10 oz. (300 g) peeled shrimp
· 10 oz. (300 g) arugula
· 1 unwaxed lemon
· ¼ cup (60 ml) extra virgin olive oil
· Salt and freshly ground pepper

A day ahead: Soak the beans in cold water for 12 hours.

Cook the beans in a pot of boiling water for a total of 45 minutes, keeping an eye on the time. After 43 minutes, drop the shrimp into the hot water and leave for 2 minutes. Drain, and allow the beans and shrimp to cool.

Wash the arugula, and dry it well. Wash the lemon and slice it into fine rounds.

Arrange the arugula in a salad bowl with the white beans, shrimp, and lemon slices.

Season with salt and pepper and drizzle with the olive oil.

OPPOSITE: On a pile of tin plates are the *castraure*, the first artichokes of the year, from the large vegetable garden.
LEFT (TOP): Preparation of artichoke bottoms. (BOTTOM): Artichoke bottoms in water.
ABOVE: In the large stone basin in the center of the vegetable garden, rainwater is collected and used to water the vegetables and the roses.

BIGOLI IN SALSA

Bigoli Pasta with Anchovy Sauce

SERVES 4

· 1 onion
· ¾ cup (200 ml) olive oil
· 8 anchovies, packed in oil
· 14 oz. (400 g) black bigoli pasta, or thick spaghetti-type pasta such as spaghettoni
· A few sprigs flat-leaf parsley, chopped

Chop the onion and sauté in the olive oil in a large skillet or pan without allowing it to color. Add 7 of the anchovies and allow them to soften until they disintegrate. Set aside the eighth anchovy for decoration.

In a large pot of boiling salted water, cook the pasta. Drain, reserving a little of the cooking liquid to mix into the anchovy sauce. Transfer the pasta into the sauce in the skillet, add some cooking liquid, and mix well. Garnish with the whole anchovy and sprinkle with the parsley.

GRANCHI ALLA VENEZIANA

Venetian-Style Crabs

SERVES 4

· 4 spider crabs or medium-sized crabs
· 2 lemons
· A few sprigs flat-leaf parsley, chopped
· ¾ cup (200 ml) olive oil
· Salt and freshly ground pepper

Holding each crab by one of the claws, rinse under running water. Place them in a pot of boiling water with half of one of the lemons. Cook for about 20 minutes; when they are bright red, they are ready.

Allow crabs to cool in the cooking water. Drain, then cut off the claws and cut the upper shell horizontally. Using a small kitchen knife, scrape out the flesh and any coral roe. Cut the flesh roughly and drizzle with the juice of half a lemon.

Return all the flesh to the shells and scatter with the chopped parsley.

Prepare a sauce: Combine the olive oil and juice of the remaining lemon. Season with salt and pepper.

Serve the crabs with the sauce on the side.

LEFT: Among the trees of the nineteenth-century park is a view of a small neoclassical temple.
FOLLOWING PAGES (LEFT): crabs left to cool off, before being cooked Venetian style; (RIGHT): Barbara Valmarana's collection of teapots adorns the mantelshelf of the 1950s-style kitchen.

BUSSOLAI BURANELLI

Biscotti di Burano
Burano Cookies

SERVES 4 OR MAKES ABOUT 2 LB. (1 KG) COOKIES
· 1¾ sticks (7 oz. / 200 g) butter, softened
· 4 cups (1 lb. 2 oz. / 500 g) all-purpose flour
· 1 cup (7 oz. / 200 g) sugar
· 5 eggs
· 2 egg yolks
· 1 sachet vanilla sugar (buy online, or substitute ½ teaspoon ground vanilla bean, or 1 teaspoon vanilla extract)

Preheat the oven to 350°F (180°C). Line a baking sheet with parchment or baking paper.
Using a wooden spoon, combine all the ingredients to make a soft dough. Roll it into log shapes.

Cut log into 3 inch-long (8 cm) pieces and shape into rings. Bake for 20 minutes, until golden.

FRITTELLE DI MELE

Apple Fritters

SERVES 4
Batter:
· 1 egg
· ¾ cup plus 2 tablespoons (3½ oz. / 100 g) all-purpose flour
· ¾ cup (200 ml) milk
· 1 drop orange flower water, or more depending on the concentration

For the fritters:
· 4 small apples
· Oil for frying
· Granulated sugar for sprinkling

Make the batter, follow the directions on page 164 for Zucchini Blossom and Herb Fritters, adding the orange flower water.

Peel and core the apples, and cut them into round slices.

Heat the oil. Dip the apple slices into the batter, and, working in batches if necessary, fry the fritters until golden.

Drain the excess oil by placing the fritters on paper towels, and sprinkle with the sugar before serving hot.

LEFT: A bridge and a path in the romantic English park of Villa Cittadella.
OPPOSITE: The apple crepes and the Burano *bussolai* are served in Murano glass dishes.

SALT

Without a doubt, the mainstay of Venetian power was salt. Since time immemorial, the people living around the lagoons have worked hard, laboring the inhospitable terrain. Salt harvesters dry, evaporate, and rake the salt, blessing the brackish water that produces their livelihood—for even gold is less in demand than salt! Around the salt pans, the mills turn and grind the fleur de sel, the delicate crust of evaporating seawater. The doge of the Republic of Venice created a monopoly for himself, controlling the Monastery of San Zaccaria, which possessed 43 salt marshes throughout the estuary. In La Giudecca and Zattere, enormous brick warehouses stored vast quantities of salt ready to be exported throughout Europe. Salt was also used to preserve meat and fish for the long voyages that La Serenissima organized to the Far East. Today, the warehouses of Zattere have been transformed into art galleries and sailing clubs. But a few artisanal salt producers are still operating in the estuaries of the Brenta, the Po, and the Adige rivers.

A residence on the Brenta river

VILLA BON TESSIER

in Mira

A round the middle of the sixteenth century, the Senate of the Venetian Republic decided to cancel the centuries-old law that reserved commerce to nobles. Many noble families decided then to invest the great wealth they had accumulated through trading with the East in other enterprises, including farms on the mainland. This was the origin of the Venetian country villa, a unique type of residence that combined aesthetic and functional requirements. Alongside the main building, a number of other buildings were erected: *barchesse*, or rustic buildings that housed workers, tools, etc; stables; dovecotes; and houses for the tenants. The park similarly combined elegant geometrical pleasure gardens with orchards and vegetable gardens. Over the course of three centuries, hundreds of villas were built in the Venetian countryside. In the early phase, the idea of the villa as a pleasure resort where one could live in contact with nature took second place to the idea of the villa as a mainly economic venture centered on intensive agriculture. It was only in the eighteenth century that the villa came to be seen primarily as a "place of delight."

Villa Bon Tessier rises on the right bank of the *naviglio del Brenta*, a branch of the Brenta river, halfway between Venice and Padua. The sixteenth-century building has two facades: the first is oriented toward the canal; the second, the main one, is oriented toward the garden. This choice makes Villa Bon Tessier a rarity, since traditionally Venetian villas prefer the main facade to face the river. Toward the late eighteenth century, a wing was added to the south, and the interiors also underwent major renovations.

Most of the hallways and rooms are still decorated with interesting eighteenth-century stucco. On the walls of the gallery on the ground floor there are a number of niches in which the allegory of seasons was painted by Costantino Cedini, an extremely productive student of Giambattista Tiepolo. Above the doors of the *portego*, the traditional Venetian salon, we can admire grisaille paintings of a group of cherubs, framed in stucco moldings over a blue background à la Wedgwood, painted by Giovanni Carlo Bevilacqua.

A dual staircase leads to the second floor; the stairway is decorated with marble-painted marmorino stucco and barrel vaults decorated with coffers and stucco roses.

The gardens are in the nineteenth-century Romantic style, with gravel paths and packed earth bordered by flowerbeds of lilies of the valley. The Tessier family has owned the villa since the early twentieth century.

BELOW: The entrance to the villa on the bank of the Brenta Canal is decorated with elegant neoclassical stucco from the late eighteenth century.
OPPOSITE: The grand dual stairway leading to the second floor of the residence. The walls and the vaults of the stairs are decorated with stucco, marble, and frescoes in Louis XVI style.

Sweet and Sour Crayfish

SERVES 4
· 3 sweet onions
· 4 to 5 tablespoons extra virgin olive oil
· ¼ cup (60 ml) white vinegar
· 1 teaspoon sugar
· 2 bay leaves
· 8 crayfish (or small scampi)
· Salt and freshly ground pepper

Prepare the marinade: Slice the onions into thin rounds, and fry them very lightly in the olive oil. Remove from the heat and add the vinegar, sugar, and bay leaves. Allow to cool for 2 hours.

Prepare the crayfish: Wash them well and place in boiling water for 3 minutes. Allow to cool in the cooking liquid. Drain and peel, and remove the heads. Cutting the shells with a pair of scissors, carefully remove the flesh.

Arrange the crayfish in a serving dish, and cover with the onion marinade. Season with salt and pepper and serve as an antipasti.

PREVIOUS DOUBLE SPREAD: The flooring in the hall is made of Venetian terazzo, made with fragments of marble or semi-precious stones.

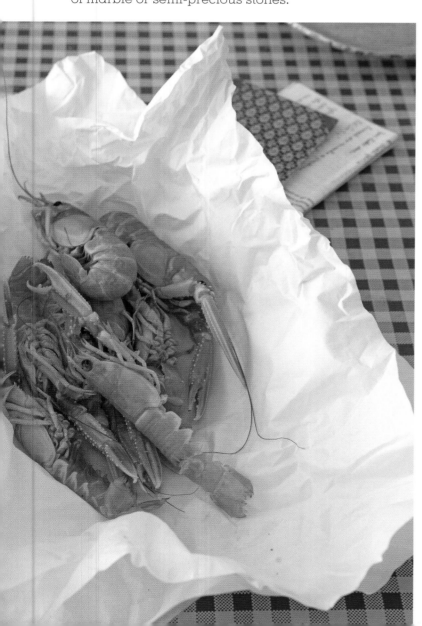

MOLECHE FRITTE

Small Fried Crabs

SERVES 4
· 3 cups (800 ml) peanut oil for frying
· 1½ lb. (700 g) *moleche*, or other soft shell crabs
· ¾ cup (100 g) flour

Moleche are small crabs found in the lagoon of Venice that are typically fried and eaten whole. They are sold at the Rialto market during January and February, when they shed their hard shell. You can use other soft shell crabs, of course.

Wash and dry the crabs carefully and roll them in the flour. Heat the oil until it is bubbling and throw the crabs into the hot oil, taking care to avoid being splattered. As soon as the crabs are golden, remove them from the oil and drain on sheets of paper towel.

Serve with polenta (see recipe on page 124).

(See photograph on the following page.)

OPPOSITE: On the bottom shelf of the central table of the kitchen, a few brass cauldrons, used to cook polenta. Little Napoleon likes to hide underneath the table for his afternoon siesta.

CAPESANTE DI CHIOGGIA

Baked Scallops

SERVES 4
· 16 small Chioggia scallops, or other scallops, on the half-shell
· Salt
· 1 bunch flat-leaf parsley, chopped
· A little extra virgin olive oil
· 1 lemon, quartered

Preheat the oven to 350°F (180°C).

Place the scallops in their shells in an ovenproof dish. Season with salt and cook in the oven for 10 minutes. Sprinkle with the chopped parsley and return to the oven to cook for an additional 10 minutes.

Just before serving, drizzle with the olive oil, and serve with the lemon wedges.

FINOCCHI AL BURRO

Butter-Braised Fennel

SERVES 4

· 4 small fennel bulbs
· 1 tablespoon (20 g) butter
· 10 sprigs dill, chopped
· A little freshly grated nutmeg

Wash the fennel bulbs and cut them into quarters. Drop them in boiling water to blanch them, then drain. Melt the butter in a skillet, add the fennel quarters with the dill, and sauté. Grate in a little nutmeg.

Cover with a lid and braise over low heat for 10 to 15 minutes. Serve as a side dish alongside fish.

You can use this recipe to prepare artichoke bottoms, sweet potatoes, or small zucchini.

BRANZINO AI CAPPERI E LIMONE

Baked Sea Bass with Capers and Lemon

SERVES 4

· 1 sea bass weighing 2 lb. (1 kg)
· 2 tablespoons capers in vinegar
· 4 garlic cloves
· 4 tablespoons extra virgin olive oil
· 1 unwaxed lemon
· 1 bunch flat-leaf parsley, chopped
· Salt and freshly ground pepper

Preheat the oven to 350°F (180°C).

Place the fish in an appropriately-sized ovenproof dish, surrounded with the capers and garlic cloves. Drizzle with the olive oil. Rinse the lemon and slice it into thin rounds. Place them over the fish, and season with salt and pepper.

Cook for 8 minutes, then reduce the oven temperature to 320°F (160°C). Sprinkle with the parsley, and bake for an additional 15 minutes.

Serve accompanied by Butter-Braised Fennel (see recipe on page 206).

PREVIOUS PAGE: The garden provides all the fruit necessary for the production of marmalade and vegetables preserved in vinegar. A collection of ancient tin plates adorns the walls of the kitchen. LEFT: An old notebook holding the family recipes is the bible of the villa. Mrs. Tessier is constantly consulting and reworking the old recipes.

PREVIOUS SPREAD: The kitchen of Villa Bon Tessier maintains its 1950s style. The wood stove is used to cook polenta.
BELOW: From the stables, where the saddles are kept, one has access to the vegetable garden.

DOLCE AL CIOCCOLATO E CARAMEI

Creamy Chocolate Dessert with Candied Fruit and Nuts

SERVES 6

Creamy Chocolate Dessert:
· 5 egg yolks
· 2 tablespoons sugar
· 4 tablespoons all-purpose flour
· 7 oz. (200 g) baking chocolate
· 4 cups (1 liter) milk

Butter a 16-inch (40 cm) cake pan.

Briskly whisk the egg yolks with the sugar until the mixture is frothy. Sift the flour and fold it in.

Melt the chocolate in a saucepan with the milk, and beat it into the egg yolks with the sugar and flour. Place the mixture in a saucepan over low heat. Stirring gently, cook until it thickens. Remove from the heat as soon as the mixture comes to a simmer.

Pour into the prepared cake pan and allow to cool to lukewarm. Turn the dessert onto a serving platter and slice.

Caramelized Dried Fruit:
· 13½ oz. (100 g) of each type of fruit—such as figs, prunes, and dates—and nuts—such as whole walnuts and almonds
· 2 lb. (1 kg) sugar
· 20 skewers

Thread an assortment of dried fruit and nuts on the skewers.

In a large pan over low heat, make a caramel with the sugar and ¾ cup (200 ml) of water. As soon as the caramel is a golden color, place two or three skewers of fruit and nuts in it, twirling them to coat the fruit and nuts. Remove, continuing to twirl to prevent threads from dropping, until the caramel sets.

Place on wax paper until completely set, and coat the fruit on the remaining skewers.

A famous Palladian villa

VILLA FOSCARI

called La Malcontenta

La Malcontenta, the only villa designed by Andrea Palladio on the Brenta River, was built for brothers Niccolò and Alvise Foscari in 1559. The building is enriched by an exceptional architectural element: a portico reproducing the facade of a Roman temple, the first architectural citation of this type in history. On the second floor, we can admire a cycle of paintings that extends over the walls and ceilings of the rooms. The cycle began to be painted immediately after the building was finished and was carried out in successive phases with the participation of several painters. Battista Franco began the cycle, and when he left it unfinished his work was taken up by Giovanni Battista Zelotti, a student of Paolo Veronese. Bernardino India also worked on the cycle, painting the smaller rooms in the grotesque style.

As centuries went by, the fate of the villa followed that of the declining Venetian Republic. In the early twentieth century, it was in a state of neglect and used as a deposit. Luckily, in 1924, Bertie Landsberg bought the building, and, assisted and advised by his friends Paul Rodocanachi and baroness Catherine d'Erlanger, began an extraordinary restoration campaign of the villa and the surrounding area. From 1924 to 1939, La Malcontenta was a lively center of international cultural and fashionable life.

Since 1973, the villa has been the property of architects Antonio and Barbara Foscari Widmann Rezzonico, who have wisely preserved the interior decoration chosen by Landsberg. They continue to take exemplary care of this beautiful place, which UNESCO has recognized as a World Heritage Site.

OPPOSITE: The majestic central hall with a frescoed vaulted ceiling is flooded with light from the windows overlooking the garden, which is reflected on the ancient Venetian pavement on the terrace.

TOP LEFT: The famous main façade of the villa, overlooking the Brenta. This Palladian model had a great influence on European and transatlantic architecture, giving rise to the Neo-Palladian style.

LEFT: Two small armchairs, covered with thick linen slipcovers, are arranged on a wooden platform. Next to them, a chair designed by Landsberg, who drew inspiration from the neoclassical chairs designed by Jappelli for Villa Cittadella (see p. 178–79) and for the caffè Pedrocchi in Padua. Jappelli himself was inspired by the *Klismos*, the famous classical Greek chairs. Architect Barbara Foscari del Vicario, too, has drawn inspiration from the chairs for her line of furniture called La Malcontenta.

ABOVE: The main door in larch wood opens onto the portico of the *pronao*, where dark green *Klismos* chairs are positioned.

PREVIOUS SPREAD: In the central lounge, on the side facing the garden, wooden architectural elements have been reused to create two reading areas.

BELOW AND RIGHT: The rooms on the ground floor, typically used as service rooms, are all vaulted and plastered in white. Presently, they are used as a kitchen and dining room by the owners. In the office, a service hatch communicates with the dining room. On an old kitchen table with tin table top, we see the vegetables from the garden. On the right, an octagonal piece of furniture, designed by Barbara Foscari, serves as a cupboard for the glasses.

BELOW: On the walls of the dining room is a dish set in black ceramic from Fratterosa, made in Urbino.
FOLLOWING PAGES: The table in the dining room is lit only by candles. Glasses are by Venini, and the octagonal candelabrum is designed by Barbara Foscari.

QUAGLIE E FUNGHI

Quails with Porcini

SERVES 8

For the quails:
· 8 quails
· 8 thin slices bacon
· 8 sage leaves
· 1 tablespoon (20 g) butter
· Scant ½ cup (100 ml) extra virgin olive oil
· Scant ½ cup (100 ml) white wine, optional
· 8 toothpicks

For the porcini:
· 1 lb. (500 g) porcini
· 3 tablespoons extra virgin olive oil
· 1 garlic clove, chopped
· 4 sprigs flat-leaf parsley

Preheat the oven to 410°F (210°C). Butter and oil a large-rimmed cooking tray.

Wrap a slice of bacon around each quail, holding them in place with a toothpick. Insert a sage leaf into the skin. Brown the quails lightly on all sides, turning them frequently. Roast for 20 to 30 minutes, taking care that they do not dry out.

Make the sauce: Pour the white wine into the cooking tray a few minutes before the quails are cooked through.

In a skillet, heat the olive oil and sauté the porcini with the clove of garlic. When they are done, sprinkle the porcini with the chopped parsley.

Serve very hot to accompany the quails.

FARAONA CON PATATE ARROSTO

Guinea Fowl with Roasted Potatoes

SERVES 4

· One 2½-lb. (1.2 kg) guinea fowl
· Scant ½ cup (100 ml) extra virgin olive oil
· 3 sprigs rosemary
· 2 lb. (1 kg) new potatoes
· Salt and freshly ground pepper

Preheat the oven to 410°F (210°C).

Brush the guinea fowl with some of the oil and place in a large ovenproof dish. Arrange the rosemary around the bird. Drizzle the potatoes with the remaining oil and dot them around the guinea fowl. Season with salt and pepper and roast in the oven for 1 hour, basting regularly.

POLENTA, FUNGHI E FORMAGGIO

Polenta with Mushrooms and Assorted Cheeses

SERVES 4

· 2 lb. (1 kg) wild mushrooms, such as chanterelle mushrooms, brown beech mushrooms, and porcini mushrooms
· 1 garlic clove
· 3 tablespoons (50 g) butter
· ½ tablespoon cornstarch or all-purpose flour
· 7 oz. (200 g) assorted cheeses, such as Fontina, Asiago, Parmigiano Reggiano, and fresh mozzarella

Clean the mushrooms under running water. Slice the oyster mushrooms, but leave the others whole.

In a skillet, sauté the whole garlic clove in the butter. Add all of the mushrooms. Reduce the heat to low and cook for about 15 minutes. If the mushrooms render too much liquid, stir in the cornstarch to thicken the sauce. Keep them warm while you prepare the polenta.

Prepare a dish of fine-grain polenta, following the recipe on page 124.

Grate the cheeses together.

Spread the grated cheese over the bottom of a large serving dish and cover with the boiling polenta. Top with the hot wild mushrooms.

LEFT: In the only bedroom on the second floor is a "Veronese" vase made of Murano glass, designed by Vittorio Zecchin in the 1920s.

Greek-Style Almond Tart

SERVES 4

· 3 eggs
· A pinch of salt
· ⅔ cup (4½ oz. / 125 g) sugar
· 1 stick plus 2 tablespoons (5 oz. / 150 g) butter, softened
· 2 cups (7 oz. / 200 g) almond flour
· Finely grated zest of 1 unwaxed lemon
· 1 roll (about ½ lb. / 250 g) puff pastry
· Confectioners' sugar for dusting

Separate the eggs. Whisk the egg whites with a pinch of salt until they hold medium peaks.

Using an electric beater, cream the sugar and butter. When the mixture is very light and fluffy, whisk in the egg yolks one by one.

Beat in the almond flour. Using a wooden spoon, carefully fold in the whipped egg whites, then stir in the lemon zest.

Place the puff pastry in an 8 x 10 inch pie dish or high-rimmed tart pan, and fill with the almond flour mixture. Bake for 40 minutes, or until golden.

Allow to cool and dust with confectioners' sugar before serving.

LEFT (TOP): The foyer on the ground floor. (BOTTOM): Detail of one of the rooms on the second floor with a large fireplace in red Verona marble.

INDEX OF RECIPES

INDEX OF SIDEBARS

LIST OF RESOURCES

GROCERY STORES

Drogheria Mascari: spices, oil, vinegar, Italian specialties
San Polo 381, Calle degli Spezieri
Tel. 041 5229762
www.imascari.com
Vaporetto stop: Rialto Mercato

PASTA

Giacomo Rizzo: all kinds of dry and fresh pasta, ravioli, dumplings, tortellini, lasagna
Cannaregio 5778, Salizada
San Giovanni Grisostomo
Tel. 041 5222824
Vaporetto stop: Rialto

BAKERY

Baldin Romina: organic bread
Cannaregio 1291, Fondamenta delle Guglie
Tel. 041 715773
Vaporetto stop: Guglie

FRUITS AND VEGETABLES

Daily markets
Mercato di Rialto
San Polo, Campo della Pescaria
Open Monday to Saturday,
7 am to 8 pm
www.veneziaunica.it/it/content/mercati

Mercato di Via Garibaldi
Castello, Via Garibaldi
Open Monday to Saturday,
7 am to 2 pm
www.veneziaunica.it/it/content/mercati

The flavors of Sant'Erasmo
Via Boaria Vecia 6, Isola di Sant'Erasmo – order by registering on the site
www.isaporidisanterasmo.com
Tel. 041 5282997 – Carlo: 3470594687 – Claudio: 3480418032

Donna Gnora
Via Mestrina 10, Noale (VE)
www.donnagnora.it
For a delivery of a box of freshly picked vegetables by boat, contact Federico – Tel. 3939719606 or email: segreteria@donnagnora.it

FISH MARKET

Rialto Fish Market
(closed on Mondays)
San Polo, Campo de le Becarie - Loggia Grande e Loggia Piccola
Covered market, from Tuesday to Saturday, 7 am to 2 pm
www.veneziaunica.it/it/content/mercati
Vaporetto stop: Rialto Mercato

CHEESES

La Baita
San Polo 47, Ruga degli Oresi
Fermata vaporetto: Rialto Mercato

WINE SELLER AND WINE BAR

Casa Mattiazzi: wines from Friuli, Marzemino, Prosecco and Pinot wines
Cannaregio 1116, Fondamenta delle Guglie
Tel. 041 5245365
Vaporetto stop: Guglie

Cantinone già Schiavi: spritz drinks, delicious wines, and Venetian *cicheti* (crostini and a range of small sandwiches, including their delicious cream of tuna with leeks).
Dorsoduro 992, Fondamenta Nani
Tel. 041 5230034
www.cantinaschiavi.com
Vaporetto stop: Zattere or Accademia

BAR PASTICCERIE

Cakes and pastries to eat in or to go, coffee and drinks at the counter
Pasticceria Rio Marin: outdoor terrace in summer
Santa Croce 784, Rio Marin
Tel. 041718523
Vaporetto stop: Riva de Biasio

Pasticceria Tonolo
Dorsoduro 3764, Calle San Pantalon
Tel. 041 5237209
pasticceria-tonolo-venezia.business.site
Vaporetto stop: San Tomà

Italo Didovich
Castello 5909, Campo Santa Marina
Tel. 041 5230017
Vaporetto stop: Rialto

Caffè del Doge
San Polo 609, Calle dei Cinque
Tel. 041 5227787
www.caffedeldoge.com
Vaporetto stop: Rialto Mercato or San Silvestro

CHOCOLATIER

Vizio Virtù
Castello 5988, Calle del Pistor
Tel. 041 2750149
www.viziovirtu.com
Vaporetto stop: Rialto

FLORIST

Mercato di Rialto
Campo de la Pescaria
Vaporetto stop: Rialto Mercato
If you're at the flower market, don't miss the stands with vendors selling jewelery, scarves, umbrellas, and raincoats.

ANTIQUES

Campo Do Pozzi di Francesco Nassivera & C. S.a.s.- Antiquariato vetri soffiati
San Polo 2581
Tel. 041 714871

RESTAURANTS

Trattoria Corte Sconta: Venetian specialties, fresh fish and seafood, fresh homemade pasta. Booking required in the evening.
Castello 3886, Calle del Pestrin
Tel. 041 5227024
www.cortescontavenezia.com
Vaporetto stop: Arsenale

Osteria Al Mascaron: traditional Venetian cuisine
Castello 5225, Calle Longa
S. Maria Formosa
Tel. 041 5225995
www.osteriamascaron.it
Vaporetto stop: Rialto

Trattoria Antica Besseta: traditional Venetian cuisine
Santa Croce 1395, Salizada de Ca' Zusto
Tel. 041 721687
Vaporetto stop: Riva de Biasio

Osteria al Cicheto: also wine bar
Cannaregio 367/a, Calle della Misericordia
Tel. 041 716037
Vaporetto stop: Ferrovia

Bistrot de Venise: restaurant, wine bar, contemporary Venetian gastronomy.
San Marco 4685, Calle dei Fabbri
Tel. 041 5236651
www.bistrotdevenise.com
Vaporetto stop: Rialto

GETTING AROUND

After visiting the islands of Murano and Burano, stop at the Trattoria Storica to taste their *tramizzini* sandwiches.
Trattoria Storica
Cannaregio 4858, Salizada Seriman
Tel. 041 5285266
www.trattoriastorica.it
Vaporetto stop: Fondamente Nove

Trattoria Alla Fontana
Cannaregio 1102, Fondamenta delle Guglie
Tel. 041 715077
Vaporetto stop: Guglie

HOTEL

Foresteria Levi
San Marco 2893, Calle Giustinian
Tel. 041 2770542
www.foresterialevi.it
Vaporetto stop: San Samuele or Accademia

Foresteria Valdese
Castello 5170, Calle Lunga
S. Maria Formosa
Tel. 041 5286797
www.foresteriavenezia.it
Vaporetto stop: Rialto or San Zaccaria

Beyond the Garden
San Polo 2542, Fondamenta Contarini
Tel. 041 2750015
www.oltreilgiardino-venezia.com
Vaporetto stop: San Tomà

Palazzo Guardi
Dorsoduro 995, Calle del Pistor
(Rio San Trovaso)
Tel. 041 2960725
www.palazzoguardivenice.com
Vaporetto stop: Accademia

The Bauer Venezia
San Marco 1459, Campo San Moisè
Tel. 041 5207022
www.bauervenezia.com
Vaporetto stop: San Marco

FOR DRINKS AND A DIFFERENT VIEW OF THE CITY

Hotel Molino Stucky
Giudecca 810
Tel. 041 2723311
www.molinostuckyhilton.it

SLEEP IN A PALAZZO OR RENT AN APARTMENT

Contact Paola Doria
Tel. 041 2411149
www.viewsonvenice.com

COSTUME ATELIER FOR CARNIVAL

Atelier Pietro Longhi
San Polo 2608, Rio Terà
By appointment: Tel. 041 714478
www.pietrolonghi.com
Vaporetto stop: San Tomà

HANDMADE CARNIVAL MASKS

Blue Moon
San Polo 1578, Calle del Capeler
Tel. 041 715175
www.bluemoonvenice.com
Vaporetto stop: Rialto Mercato

TAKE A RIDE IN A GONDOLA

Tel. 041 5287075
www.gondolavenezia.it

TAKE A CRUISE ON THE BRENTA TO VIEW THE PALLADIAN VILLAS

Il Burchiello
Via Porciglia, 34
35121 Padova
Tel. 049 8760233
www.ilburchiello.it
info@ilburchiello.it

VISIT VILLA FOSCARI, LA MALCONTENTA

La Malcontenta srl.
Via dei Turisti 9
30034 Malcontenta di Mira (VE)
Tel. 041 5470012 (041 5203966)
Open from April to October 31, Tuesday and Saturday 9 am to 12 pm
www.lamalcontenta.com
info@lamalcontenta.com

ACKNOWLEDGMENTS

The publisher and the authors wish to thank all
owners of the residences described in this volume,
who opened the doors of their homes and shared
their precious family recipes.

For the French Edition:
Editor in Chief: Valérie Tognali
Editor: Aude Le Pichon
Artistic Director: Sabine Houplain, assisted by Claire Mieyeville
Graphic Design: Isabelle Ducat
Copy Editor: Valérie Mettais
Production: Marion Lance
Sales: Mathilde Barrois
Public Relations: Hélène Maurice

For the US Edition:
Project Editor: Jennifer Duardo
Translation of recipes and sidebars from French to English:
Carmella Abramowitz Moreau
Translation of main texts and captions from Italian to English:
Gabriele Poole
Typesetting: Kayleigh Jankowski
Copy Editor: Julie Schumacher

First published in the United States of America in 2018 by
Rizzoli International Publications, Inc.
300 Park Avenue South
New York, NY 10010
www.rizzoliusa.com

Originally published in French in 2016 by Hachette Livre

© 2016 Éditions du Chêne – Hachette Livre

2018 2019 2020 2021 / 10 9 8 7 6 5 4 3 2 1

ISBN: 978-0-8478-6182-8

Library of Congress Control Number: 2017954611

Printed in China